The Year of the Poet X

April 2023

The Poetry Posse

inner child press, ltd.

The Poetry Posse 2023

Gail Weston Shazor
Shareef Abdur Rasheed
Teresa E. Gallion
hülya n. yılmaz
Kimberly Burnham
Tzemin Ition Tsai
Elizabeth Esguerra Castillo
Jackie Davis Allen
Joe Paire
Caroline 'Ceri' Nazareno
Ashok K. Bhargava
Alicja Maria Kuberska
Swapna Behera
Albert 'Infinite' Carrasco
Michelle Joan Barulich
Eliza Segiet
William S. Peters, Sr.

~ * ~

In order to maintain each poet's authentic voice, this volume has not undergone the scrutiny of editing. Please take time to indulge each contributor for their own creativity and aspirations to convey their uniqueness.

hülya n. yılmaz, Ph.D.
Director of Editing ~
Inner Child Press International

General Information

The Year of the Poet X
April 2023 Edition

The Poetry Posse

1st Edition : 2023

Publisher Information

1st Edition : Inner Child Press
intouch@innerchildpress.com
www.innerchildpress.com

ISBN-13 : 978-1-952081-95-8 (inner child press, ltd.)

$ 12.99

WHAT WOULD
LIFE
BE WITHOUT
A LITTLE
POETRY?

Dedication

This Book is dedicated to

Humanity, Peace & Poetry

the Power of the Pen

can effectuate change!

&

The Poetry Posse

past, present & future,

our Patrons and Readers &

the Spirit of our Everlasting Muse

In the darkness of my life
I heard the music
I danced . . .
and the Light appeared
and I dance

Janet P. Caldwell

Table of Contents

The Poetry Posse

Table of Contents . . . *continued*

Foreword

Children: Difference Makers

Claudette Colvin

The Poetry Posse Family has another gift to offer for the April 2023 Issue: The Power of Justice and how Claudette Colvin lived to see that change.

Claudette Colvin really proved that all of us should stand for it; she posted, ‘’I knew then, and I know now that, when it comes to justice, there is no easy way to get it. You can't sugarcoat it. You have to take a stand and say, 'This is not right.'

Mary Jane Gadson and C. Austin gave birth to Claudette Colvin on September 5, 1939, in Montgomery, Alabama, USA.

According to many online resources, Colvin attended the city's segregated Booker T. Washington High School in 1955. Her family didn't own a car, so she had to rely on the city's buses to go to and from school. Although African Americans made up the majority of passengers on the bus system, they were subjected to discrimination due to the system's practice of segregated seating. Colvin had been studying the civil rights movement in school and was a part of the NAACP Youth Council. She was forcibly removed from the bus and arrested by the two policemen because she refused to give up her place on the bus.

The arrest of Parks, another woman who nine months after Colvin, received a lot of attention in writing about the civil rights movement in Montgomery. Colvin's narrative has received little attention, in contrast to Parks, who has been hailed as a civil rights hero. Several people have made changes to that. The poem "Claudette Colvin Goes to Work" by Rita Dove was eventually turned into a song.

In the young adult biography Claudette Colvin: Twice Toward Justice, Phillip Hoose wrote a detailed account of her life, published in 2009. He claimed that he wanted the general public to be aware of the 15-year-old because, in reality, without his initial cry for freedom, Rosa Parks and Dr. King would not have existed.

Claudette Colvin became an American pioneer of the 1950s civil rights movement and retired nurse aide. Colvin assisted in advancing civil rights initiatives in Montgomery, despite the fact that her contribution to the struggle to remove segregation there may not be publicly acknowledged. "Claudette inspired moral courage in all of us; if she had not done what she did.''

Claudette Colvin and many more unsung heroes may be forgotten, but their legacies live on and see how society changed for the better.

Caroline 'Ceri Naz' Nazareno Gabis

Preface

We, **Inner Child Press International, The Year of the Poet** and **The Poetry Posse** welcome you.

We are so excited as we are now offer unto you our fourth month of our **10th** year of monthly publication of this enterprise, **The Year of the Poet**. For those of you who are not familiar with our story, back in 2013, a few of us poets got together with the simple intention of producing a book a month. That was our challenge. Since that time the enterprise has blossomed and brought forth a fruit that seems to keep on growing as evidenced as we enter 2023.

Our purpose is simple. Through our lyrical words and verse, we not only wish to share our poetic works, but we also have the poetic naiveté to believe that we can assist in the growth of consciousness of the things that have an effect our collective humanity. Therefore, we welcome your readership. For more about what we are attempting to accomplish, have a look at our Publishing Web Site . . . www.innerchildpress.com. If you would like to know a bit more about this particular endeavor please stop by for a visit at :
www.innerchildpress.com/the-year-of-the-poet

Over the years, Inner Child Press has been socially active to bring awareness and catalog through literature the things that have an impact upon our world and its inhabitants. We have solicited, produced, underwritten and published quite a few volumes to that end. For more insight you may wish to visit : www.innerchildpress.com/the-anthology-market. If you are a writer, poet, or activist, you would be advised to keep a eye out for upcoming volumes should you desire to participate. All readers are welcomed as well. Note, that there is a myriad of published volumes that are available as a FREE PDF download as well as available for purchase at affordable prices.

We at this time extend to you our well wishes for your own personal journey and hope that you consider including us as a travel companion.

Bless Up

Bill

william s. peters, sr.
Poet, Writer, Activist, Humanitarian

William S. Peters, Sr.

Publisher
Inner Child Press International
www.innerchildpress.com

Children

Difference Makers

Claudette Colvin

April 2023

by Kimberly Burnham, Ph.D.

Colvin was 15 when she became a major player in the Civil Rights Movement by refusing to give up her bus seat to a caucasian rider. This was nine months before Rosa Parks was arrested for the same thing. She was one of the four plaintiffs involved in the Supreme Court case that ultimately outlawed segregation on Alabama buses. Colvin has said about her experience, "I feel very, very proud of what I did. I do feel like what I did was a spark and it caught on."

"I felt like Sojourner Truth was pushing down on one shoulder and Harriet Tubman was pushing down on the other, saying, 'Sit down girl!' I was glued to my seat."

—Claudette Colvin

Poets . . .
sowing seeds in the
Conscious Garden of Life,
that those who have yet to come
may enjoy the Flowers.

Poets, Writers . . . know that we are the enchanting magicians that nourishes the seeds of dreams and thoughts . . . it is our words that entice the hearts and minds of others to believe there is something grand about the possibilities that life has to offer and our words tease it forth into action . . . for you are the Poet, the Writer to whom the Gift of Words has been entrusted . . .

~ wsp

Poetry succeeds where instruction fails.

~ wsp

Now Available

Inner Child Press International

&

The Year of the Poet

present

Poetry

the best of 2022

innerchildpressanthologies@gmail.com

Gail
Weston
Shazor

This is a creative promise ~ my pen will speak to and for the world. Enamored with letters and respectful of their power, I have been writing for most of my life. A mother, daughter, sister and grandmother I give what I have been given, greatfilledly.

Author of . . .

"An Overstanding of an Imperfect Love"
&
Notes from the Blue Roof

Lies My Grandfathers Told Me

available at Inner Child Press.

www.facebook.com/gailwestonshazor
www.innerchildpress.com/gail-weston-shazor
navypoet1@gmail.com

Musical Chairs

The wheels on the bus go round and round
I am tired and I need to sit down
All day long, I have worked in the town
Time to go home and not hear a sound
And you like you trying to get wound
Imma get on this bus after paying my pound
Of flesh that's required mostly around
These parts of the world that's underground
You have no idea what my life is about
Sun up to sun down with little money to count
Your looks and your voices need to get the hell out
Cause right here imma gone sit down
While the wheels on this bus go round

Listen, Listen

Y'all better listen quick
Somebody trying to learn
You something
It ain't when they got you
That you in trouble
Cause another man done gone
From the county farm
The gate was left just a bit ajar
Just a bit so he could see
And the others said
Nah man
This is protective custody
In here we safe
And they waited for the feeding time
Stuff slid under the door
Thrown over the fence
To keep everyone from roaring
The only bit of lightness
Was the complexion of the hand
They had been trained not to bite
But the door called out
Swinging gently on its rusty hinge
Singing slyly and waiting
Freedom oh freedom
Was its plaintive plea
And he knew the sun actually shone
Beyond this protection
Because he had been there
Free
From the county farm
The chains had been left long enough
Just so he could walk, text and surf

Gone were the days of hoops
And playgrounds on the corner
Time spent listening to learned ones
Listen, Listen
There is no razor wire up top
And he gave himself away
Until no one knew who he was
They didn't know his name
In the factories built on paddies
Just another Joe
The tables had been turned on
Turntables
From which prophets speak
Was that the music
Or just the others
Nah man
This is where it's at
And they turn the volume up louder
Another man done gone
Another man done gone
Awaken to the message
Of the leaders voices but it
Ain't you
Because you too scared of the song
The gate is whispering to you
Third eye close to the call
Of the drumbeat
And you won't be the man
That they kill
For running away
Because they got you tracked
GPS
Smartphones
Chips in everything you bought

Listen, Listen
Another man done gone
I didn't know his name
He had broken the long chain
Slipped through the gate
Found out who he was
And tried to save you
But you chose to stay in protective custody
They killed another man
Another brother done gone
Into the network.

On this Beach

They arrived on this beach
On this beach shoeless
The tears done and grim
For that had already been shed
On the journey
And in it's place
A stoic waiting on the next

They gripped the rags and tatters
Rags and tatters that make
Them all look the same
Dark skinned
And dirt skinned
And none knowing the where
That they are

And the new ones are restless
Ones are restless
Born in between then and now
There is no belonging
To anywhere
No official passport
Or certificates to name them

Numbered up quickly against waves
Quickly against waves
And no one will stop to count grains
Drops spilled in water
And the predators
Have left their shallowness
For places in sand

And the drums continued to beat
Continued to beat the count
So that they knew just how many
Were thrown over
The hulls of whitewashed
Soulless hulls bobbing
In the surf

When I find myself on the edge
On the edge of the water
I can hear their cries
Because the matter of the world
Has not changed
The sand remains
The same grain

As countless as the stars in the sky
The stars in the sky shine
And as you lift up your eyes
Remember
That that happened
Under your feet and you stand
On holy ground

Alicja
Maria
Kuberska

Alicja Maria Kuberska

Alicja Maria Kuberska – awarded Polish poetess, novelist, journalist, editor.

She is a member of the Polish Writers Associations in Warsaw, Poland and IWA Bogdani, Albania. She is also a member of directors' board of Soflay Literature Foundation, Our Poetry Archive (India) and Cultural Ambassador for Poland (Inner Child Press, USA)

Her poems have been published in numerous anthologies and magazines in : Poland, Czech Republic, Slovakia, Hungary,Ukraina, Belgium, Bulgaria, Albania, Spain, the UK, Italy, the USA, Canada, the UK, Argentina, Chile, Peru, Israel, Turkey, India, Uzbekistan, South Korea, Taiwan, China, Australia, South Africa, Zambia, Nigeria

She received two medals - the Nosside UNESCO Competition in Italy (2015) and European Academy of Science Arts and Letters in France (2017). Ahe also received a reward of international literary competition in Italy „ Tra le parole e 'elfinito" (2018). She was announced a poet of the 2017 year by Soflay Literature Foundation (2018).She also received : Bolesław Prus Prize Poland (2019), Culture Animator Poland (2019) and first prize Premio Internazionale di Poesia Poseidonia- Paestrum Italy (2019).

Sparkle

The first, the second, the third…
The last spark ignited the fire
Old rules and customs were burned

The space in minds widened
There are no divisions and segregation
Each ticket gives the same rights

As if nothing has changed
Longleaf pines grow and camellias bloom
But an old bus rolled into a new era

An Exhibit From The Wałbrzych Museum

Rocks excavated from the depths
of the Carboniferous forest
remember many sunrises and sunsets
The black stone releases ancient energy.

Time has put its seals on the homogeneous mass
but it retained several giant ferns
- imprinted the boughs
and great feathery leaves.

An arthropod writhes in a museum display case.
Once there were thousands, two survived.
I admire a piece of coal
more valuable than gold.

My Homeland - Poland

My homeland has a red color
like a field full of poppies among cereals
- they are drops of blood
in the fragility of the petals
and lyrics about Monte Cassino

My homeland sounds
like the clatter of storks on the roof,
Chopin notes in the willows
and the rustle of the hussar wings.

My homeland smells like a loaf of bread,
linden flowers in the garden,
sea breeze on the shores of the Baltic Sea
and the gunpowder.

My homeland means
faithfulness to the word
courage and dedication
tough love
and nameless soldier crosses

Jackie
Davis
Allen

Jackie Davis Allen

Jackie Davis Allen, otherwise known as Jacqueline D. Allen or Jackie Allen, grew up in the Cumberland Mountains of Appalachia. As the next eldest daughter of a coal miner father and a stay at home mother, she was the first in her family to attend and graduate from college. Her siblings, in their own right, are accomplished, though she is the only one, to date, that has discovered the gift of writing.

Graduating from Radford University, with a Bachelor's of Science degree in Early Education, she taught in both public and private schools. For over a decade she taught private art classes to children both in her home and at a local Art and Framing Shop where she also sold her original soft sculptured Victorian dolls and original christening gowns.

She resides in northern Virginia with her husband, taking much needed get-aways to their mountain home near the Blue Ridge Mountains, a place that evokes memories of days spent growing up in the Appalachian Mountains.

A lover of hats, she has worn many. Following marriage to her college sweetheart, and as wife, mother, grandmother, teacher, tutor, artist, writer, poet and crafter, she is a lover of art and antiques, surrounding herself, always, with books, seeking to learn more.

In 2015 she authored *Looking for Rainbows, Poetry, Prose and Art*, and in 2017, *Dark Side of the Moon*. Both books of mostly narrative poetry were published by Inner Child Press and were edited by hulya n. yilmaz in 2019, *No Illusions. Through the Looking Glass*, which was nominated to be considered for a Pulitzer Prize by the publisher and editor of Inner Child Press, ltd.

http://www.innerchildpress.com/jackie-davis-allen.php
jackiedavisallen.com

Fulfillment

Did she dream about it?

For how long?
Did she think for days before doing it?
Did she tell anyone?
Had she any nightmares?

Did she wake up in fear?

On the day to the fulfillment,
What fears had she cast aside?
In the making and carrying out her plan,
Had she considered the consequences?

Who knows what relief she felt

When she finally sat down?
Was it even a plan?
With the weight of the burden released,
She was sure that this first step was the right one.

Consequences or not, she could say:

I have made a difference!
And, if to no one else, night and day,
I am proud of myself!
I like what I see in the mirror.

One Might Say...

It is such a simple thing,
Mount the steps, drop in your coins,
Take a seat, rest your weary feet.

That's what those two teenagers did!

The ones sitting on the bench-seat,
In the back of the bus.
Did they not know, understand

That that seat and the others in the back

Are reserved for those who look like me?
Do they not know that is where
I am supposed to sit? No matter that our coins,

Each dropped in the slot, have the same value.

Earned by earnest labor, mine, theirs. Always,
The rules understood and obeyed, by one teen.
But not obeyed on that day. Neither by the other two.

And, so, I sat down near the middle of the bus.

Today, thank you, I sit where I want.
Other than the color of our skin,
We three teenagers are very much alike.

Choices

Heavy weights of dissension
Like those under contemplation
Have simmered. Some, a decade or more.

Of silence, of recriminations,
There are some willing. Some unwilling,
To change the choices made.

To forgive. To accept. Or Not?
To live in harmony? Why do we not claim
Accept pardon? Kindness? Grace?

Riding along with the tempest
Love imploringly longs to embrace,
To tenderly share healing caresses.

Intentional forgiveness is the sunshine
That guides the best of our days and ways.
With care, it improves perspective.

When love is allowed to make the choice,
The moon, the stars and the heavens celebrate.
Should we not choose to do the same?

Tzemin Ition Tsai

Tzemin Ition Tsai

Dr. Tzemin Ition Tsai comes from the Republic of China(Taiwan). In addition to being a professor of literature at a university, he is more committed to writing poems, novels, and proses. He is also an editor of "Reading, Writing and Teaching" academic text, an International editor of "Contemporary dialogues" literary periodical in Macedonia, and Vice-Chairman of the International Jury of the SAHITTO INTERNATIONAL AWARD in Bangladesh, and a columnist for "Chinese Language Monthly" in Taiwan.

In a wide range of literary creations, he is particularly fond of interesting stories or novels, and writing articles or poems about the feelings of nature and human beings. He has won many national literary awards. His literary works have been anthologized and published in books, journals, and newspapers in more than 55 countries and have been translated into more than 24 languages.

The Dark Black Comely Foal On The Road

The longer you leave your hometown, the more you get used to conquering the world
An inexplicable?
A kind of thinking?
The chaotic mountains in front of us are more of an obstacle

Horseshoe trots lightly into the village
Drizzle
The cock crows intermittently
No matter how cold it is in January, the plum and willow will not wake up
The yellow mud road slab makes the bridge inclined

Today, the newly created southern road turns around
The intermittent rosy clouds accompany the distant mountains to see off the clouds
It makes people suspicious, there are gods living in Maple Leaf Harbor, showing auspiciousness
Don't let the road back be as difficult as it used to be
Elevated far-sighted high and low

When the sun shines, the mountains gradually warm up
Returning home, going out of the valley, entering the valley, turning around
Dodging the forest and passing through the village, the mountains in Lion Township overlap and then dissolve
The birds have flown far away, the scenery is different from each other
Not to mention
My hero is never old

Cold Moon On The Lonely Castle

The moonlight hangs high in a corner of the ancient city
white, proud, and boundless
How many hardships the survivors have faced over the past century
melancholy
Frosty weather patterns in Hengchun
In the past, the surrounding city and river were bustling like a forest
Thorns grow in darkness today
Do you want to wash away the dust in your mind?

The four walls of the ancient castle are insulated from the cold
Red Mansion Rain Last Night
Reappear that splendor
Everything is a dream
The lonely lamp next to the Red House
Illuminating the high wall of red sand, the cry of the yellow oriole has not been heard in the distance for a long time

Ascend to the heights
The top of the city is gorgeous and still silent, the sunset remains the same
This is not a restaurant
Can't stop a group of friends
Sitting on the ground and drinking strong wine, indulge in the dark sky
Deliberately make that spring rebel
Raise your glass and wait for the cock to crow

As Far As The Eye Can See

The corner of the south potential, as far as the eye can see
A little autumn light forgets everything
The red rain on the green land should be the spring, and the beautiful flowers are like this
Outside the setting sun
The crow crosses back, and the smoke and water are vast
Dream soul does not reach the river

I still remember the old gulls and herons
Trees by the lake, recalling the past, accompanied by wind and dew
Let's talk about eternity
Those fragments of sentences on the broken stele, can you still remember the vicissitudes of life several times in a hundred years?
My eyes are infinitely sad, I don't see the sails hanging in the evening light

Revisiting a fallen hero
Empty sigh, sad, ecstasy, desolate
Only the end of the world
That's sad than happy

The west wind blows, and dreams turn to ashes
After a sad farewell, how can he remember him even more?
Drums are guarded at dusk, and there are a few traces of crying in the ruins of wild shops
Weeping poplar bank
The thoughts of sending pedestrians to autumn gradually fade away, but the tears are full of sleeves
Rain cloud

The lonely big bird screamed loudly
Several times
The end of the world is full of luxuriant grasses, sad and sad
Regain the Lazy Colored Pen
Write the screen of the mountain, draw its corners
There are mandarin ducks and brocade characters in the new makeup
Butterfly light silk

Shareef Abdur Rasheed

Shareef Abdur-Rasheed, AKA Zakir Flo was born and raised in Brooklyn, New York. His education includes Brooklyn College, Suffolk County Community College and Makkah, Saudi Arabia. He is a Veteran of the Viet Nam era, where in 1969 he reverted to his now reverently embraced Islamic Faith. He is very active in the Islamic community and beyond with his teachings, activism and his humanity.

Shareef's spiritual expression comes through the persona of "Zakir Flo" . Zakir is Arabic for "To remind". Never silent, Shareef Abdur-Rasheed is always dropping science, love, consciousness and signs of the time in rhyme.

Shareef is the Patriarch of the Abdur-Rasheed Family with 9 Children (6 Sons and 3 Daughters) and 41 Grandchildren (24 Boys and 17 Girls).

For more information about Shareef, visit his personal FaceBook Page at :

https://www.facebook.com/shareef.abdurrasheed1
https://zakirflo.wordpress.com

Claudette Courageous

stood up by sitting down
03/02/1955
in the town actually city
on a bus in deep
racist south
15-year-old Claudette
sat down on a bus
in Montgomery, Alabama
while being black
she sat where they said
she can't
she said i could and did
9 months before Rosa
Parks did likewise
Claudette took the prize
arrested for daring to sit
where they said only
other folk who didn't
look like her belong
sister Rosa got the press
9 months later
she launched a movement
racist south nightmare
Rosa, Claudette no fear
Claudette had baggage
carrying child out of wedlock
too much to make her the face
of a movement
Rosa got the nod
none the less young sister
became one of four plaintiffs
first federal court case

filled by civil rights attorney
Fred Grey 02/01/1956
challenge bus segregation
in Montgomery
victory 06/13/1956
3 judge panel ruled
racist policy unconstitutional
went all the way to the top
U.S. Supreme Court up held it
like a boy named Daoud vs.
the giant slew that big old giant
turns out a 15-year-old girl
name Claudette got a W
vs. racist giant Alabama
in 1956
some are chosen heed the call
run the race victorious

Clifford Brown..,

died yesterday 58 yesterdays
June 26 1956 yesterday
they called him brownie
that's what Benny Golson said
fondly remembering Clifford.
shinning bright in the middle
of Be Bops blight H filled nights
jazzmen living life on a tight wire
playing Russian roulette
laying bets on the trigger
squeezed next might be the
last and best
while blowing cooool jazzy
blue, hard bop sets
brownie sat out that nod set
blew that horn hot but horse,
scag was not in his mix
living clean was Clifford's stick
but he died not quite yet 26
on a wet night near Philly
and Benny Golson remembered
"Brownie" fondly, warmly
said "I was gigging at the Apollo
when they told me
just before our set went on in
Harlem, uptown
and we had to go on still get
it on and drown out the pain"
with that same refrain all the
time remembering Clifford just
died in the rain

Dizzy, Freddie, Lee, Miles, Mingus,
Monk, Art, Max, Sonny did the same
Clifford Brown, remember the sound . . .
remember the name

peace..,

don't come easy even when summer's breezy warmth
squeezes me
birds ' n ' bees intrigue me all food for soul that feeds me
but in the midst of it is evil elements lurk in shadows
lord only knows what evil flows from realms unknown
waiting to pounce at the right time to spoil what peace
derived
from lord's mercy bestowed in the beauty that glows
from array of creations we've come to know though
mankind's
gratitude is slow as his attitude grows cold
as the seconds, minutes come and go
his arrogance shows
so in the heat of summer's glow we all too often come to
know
mindless violence blows up peaceful silence
such is the evil one's science designed to eradicate peace
' n ' quiet, love, harmony gives way to mayhem hummin
an
evil hymn
yes this is also what summer brings in
such is modern civilization that has a penchant for
self-annihilation what the hell is wrong with lord's
humankind creation seemingly on the verge of massive
purge?
my lord have mercy.

Ameen

Kimberly
Burnham

Kimberly Burnham

A brain health expert with a PhD in Integrative Medicine, Kimberly Burnham has lived in tropical Colombia; in Belgium during the Vietnam War; in Japan teaching businessmen English; in diverse international Toronto, Canada; and several places in the US. Now, she's in Spokane, WA with her wife, Elizabeth, two sets of twins (age 11 & 14) and three dogs. Her recent book, *Awakenings: Peace Dictionary, Language and the Mind, a Daily Brain Health Program* includes the word for peace in hundreds of languages. Her poetry weaves through 80+ volumes of *The Year of the Poet*, *Inspired by Gandhi*, *Women Building the World*, and *A Woman's Place in the Dictionary*. She is currently working on several ekphrastic writing projects. One is a novel, *Art Thief Cracks Healing Code for Parkinson's Disease* and the other is non-fiction, *Using Ekphrastic Fiction Writing and Poetry to Create Interest and Promote Artists, Writers, and Poets*.

http://www.NerveWhisperer.Solutions

https://healthy-brain.medium.com/bears-at-the-window-of-climate-change-d1fb403eeaf3

One Girl on a Bus

Claudette Colvin sat
still more a spark a leader
refuse to be less

Children Lead

One leads a movement
listening to past giants one
scared child seated shines

15-Year-Old Vs Supreme Court

No one say I am
only one, too young, too old
See Be Powerful

Elizabeth

E.

Castillo

Elizabeth Esguerra Castillo

Elizabeth Esguerra Castillo is a multi-awarded and an Internationally-Published Contemporary Author/Poet and a Professional Writer / Creative Writer / Feature Writer / Journalist / Travel Writer from the Philippines. She has 2 published books, "Seasons of Emotions" (UK) and "Inner Reflections of the Muse", (USA). Elizabeth is also a co-author to more than 60 international anthologies in the USA, Canada, UK, Romania, India. She is a Contributing Editor of Inner Child Magazine, USA and an Advisory Board Member of Reflection Magazine, an international literary magazine. She is a member of the American Authors Association (AAA) and PEN International.

Web links:

Facebook Fan Page

https://free.facebook.com/ElizabethEsguerraCastillo

Google Plus

https://plus.google.com/u/0/+ElizabethCastillo

Colvin, The Unsung Heroine

This fragile girl was an unsung heroine
At a young age, she stood up for her rights
Full of courage, bravery and might
She advised young people to not give up on her dreams
At a tender age, her fearless personality shines
Colvin, an icon of the Civil Rights Movement
Though she experienced discrimination because of her color
Her contributions must be recognized with valor.

The Road to Utopia

I trekked on this vast arid land without a definite destination
Conquered the seas, climbed the highest mountain peak
Seeking a sacred haven here on earth
A place where my yearning soul truly belongs,
Fell many times along the road
But got up on my feet once more
Just to reach that sanctuary where I long to be.
A weary heart, exhausted body
But my soul refused to give up
To discover what I was looking for
Met various people along the way,
Some wicked ones who don't believe in what I say
I won't let these enemies win
Their evil mockeries won't shake my will.
Is it a sin to chase what my heart truly desires?
Could the heavens open up its doors just to whisper
To my ears where is the right path to follow?
Could there be someone out there,
To act as my blessed Guide
Calm my spirit when I grow weary
Encourage me when I feel disheartened.
And so I traversed the road to my own utopia
As angels try to console me singing hymns of a cheerful melody
I can see from the far horizon my future is finally dawning upon me,
A streak of colorful hues envelopes my being
When a rainbow after the rains suddenly illuminated my dark path
Heaven is just waiting for me out there
Looking at myself at my reflection by the lake I told myself, "This is the place where I really belong."

My Kind of Phenomenal Woman

Your words imprint a lasting effect on our minds
The immortal messages still linger in our thoughts
Your intricate and evocative verses
still echo even in the wilderness.
Your name itself is legendary, angelic
You are my kind of phenomenal woman
A woman of substance, a woman empowering other women
You moved the world with your mighty pen.
You are my kind of phenomenal woman
A great inspiration you have bestowed upon mankind
Even if years would go by, your words will remain forever in our hearts
For these have become part of our existence.

Joe Paire

Joe Paire

Joseph L Paire' aka Joe DaVerbal Minddancer . . . is a quiet man, born in a time where civil liberties were a walk on thin ice. He's been a victim of his own shyness often sidelined in his own quest for love. He became the observer, charting life's path. Taking note of the why, people do what they do. His writings oft times strike a cord with the dormant strings of the reader. His pen the rosined bow drawn across the mind. He comes full-frontal or in the subtlest way, always expressing in a way that stimulate the senses.

www.facebook.com/joe.minddancer

Nine Months

I've never heard of Claudette Colvin!
Isn't funny how history hides itself
She was the first to refuse to give up her seat
Nine months later, Rosa Parks was most noted
For doing the same thing herself.

History repeats, misery lingers on
Neither women felt defeat, their stories carry on
It's hard to tell a tale with little or no experience
It's even harder these days,
with histories disappearance

The civil rights movement needed a catalyst
A fifteen-year-old young women wasn't having it
Giving up her seat, just because of prejudice
Claudette Colvin refused!
And honestly, I'm glad she did!

It's sad that we had to struggle for basic rights
I'm wondering how such religious folk,
even slept at night
we still fight for the freedoms promised to us
the only thing we gained in life was just more ways to
screw us.

But she knew this, those before and after knew this
Now that you've had a chance to view this
Keep in mind, to some those where good times
And to erase that history is ludicrous

Sowing Seeds

Stowed away for the winter hibernation
It's so beautiful when, March winds signal changes
Red wings and a distinctive beak
I knew at first glance a Cardinal would soon speak

Just yesterday I saw one, along with its mate
Today I saw bright yellow leaves
near the fence by the gate

Spring is here, the dogwoods have already sprung
Daffodils have come and gone
Plucked by hands of a five-year-old girl
To her they're just pretty fun

Pretty sunsets as the days grow longer
I long for the rain, and days of thunder
April showers, bring mayflowers
And the Mayflower brought many things

I'm no dancer, but I tell you what
I love singing in the rain
I love to know if I like butter,
By the dandelion near my chin

My heart is set on a garden
With more than one crop of squash
I've given myself a pardon
I was jailed for the lack of heart

Tomatoes and basil, cucumbers, and potatoes
I'm going to grow a meal, with plenty for the table

Acrylic Art

With nature as a backdrop
My easel felt at home
I gently moved my fan brush
When clouds and land did form

A palette knife for images of wood
I'll carve its bark with a touch of red
Take a chance it'll blend out good

Artistic license taken, free from numbered borders
It's okay to do a numbers thing
But this scene deserves less order

Water based paint, eases the cleaning process
I've dabbled in oils once before
But to me it just felt heartless, but I'm no artist

I just speak through colors
I just speak through the coverage of my canvass
I just speak through the shadows of my madness

The color of my sadness is bolder than my smile
The color of trauma from thoughts of a child
The color of calm, from a knowing mother's wiles

I paint acrylic images
I paint my lifelong scrimmages
I feel my choices are limitless
With the ease of my easel
I'm as free as an eagle
Fly on pretty bird, let your art free you!

hülya

n.

yılmaz

hülya n. yılmaz

Professor Emerita, hülya n. yılmaz is a published author, literary translator, and Co-Chair and Director of Editing Services at Inner Child Press International. Her poetic work appeared in numerous anthologies of global endeavors and was presented at various literary events in the U.S. and abroad. In 2018, WIN honored yılmaz with an award of excellence. Since 2017, her two poems remain permanently installed in *Telepoem Booth* – a U.S.-wide poetic art exhibition. hülya finds it vital for everyone to seek a deeper sense of self, and writes creatively to attain a comprehensive awareness for and development of our humanity.

hülya n. yılmaz, a traveler on the journey called "life" . . .

Writing Web Site
https://hulyanyilmaz.com/

Editing Web Site
https://hulyasfreelancing.com

Equal Treatment

In Montgomery, Alabama of 1955 . . .

an order came about. For her arrest.
She was 15.

At that young age, Claudette Colvin
already knew the right from the wrong:
On her ride in a crowded bus,
she refused to give up her seat
to a white woman.

Her calm resistance made history
as the Montgomery Bus Boycott.
To many of us, the fame for the same
belongs to Rosa Parks.
Parks was 42 when her bus boycott
followed that of Colvin's 9 months later.

Both women demanded equal treatment;
not bowing down
before a blatant
melanin-based discrimination.

What does age matter?

Check out this volume from cover to cover,
and witness yourself the 15-year-old's impact.

Swings, See-Saws, and Such

While the most of us dreamed of plays and playgrounds
as a child, a few little ones
etched a mark into history.

Swings, see-saws, and such
probably never meant much.

The role and function of a prodigy
seem to have come to them
as naturally as their now world-renowned surnames.

Swings, see-saws, and such
are only for the ordinary bunch.

tagging along

empaths feel they do

sense a child's gut-wrenching wail

their hearts, in glass shards

Teresa E. Gallion

Teresa E. Gallion was born in Shreveport, Louisiana and moved to Illinois at the age of 15. She completed her undergraduate training at the University of Illinois Chicago and received her master's degree in Psychology from Bowling Green State University in Ohio. She retired from New Mexico state government in 2012.

She moved to New Mexico in 1987. While writing sporadically for many years, in 1998 she started reading her work in the local Albuquerque poetry community. She has been a featured reader at local coffee houses, bookstores, art galleries, museums, libraries, Outpost Performance Space, the Route 66 Festival in 2001 and the State of Oklahoma's Poetry Festival in Cheyenne, Oklahoma in 2004. She occasionally hosts an open mic.

Teresa's work is published in numerous Journals and anthologies. She has two CDs: *On the Wings of the Wind* and *Poems from Chasing Light*. She has published three books: *Walking Sacred Ground, Contemplation in the High Desert* and *Chasing Light.*

Chasing Light was a finalist in the 2013 New Mexico/Arizona Book Awards.

The surreal high desert landscape and her personal spiritual journey influence the writing of this Albuquerque poet. When she is not writing, she is committed to hiking the enchanted landscapes of New Mexico. You may preview her work at

http://bit.ly/1aIVPNq or ***http://bit.ly/13IMLGh***

A Spark for Civil Rights

Claudette, you were a spark
that ignited a flame to move.
The time had come to initiate
the right of refusal to give up
your seat on the bus.

As an adolescent, you took a stance
against fear and the threat
of aniliation for being colored.

You started a wave that Rosa rode on
in the battle for civil rights.
Your stance was much bigger than
you could imagine at age 15.

Blended Smoothie

Walking the path of the seeker
on the gravel road,
I notice the butterflies
fly in heart formations around me.

I realize I am sheltered
from negative vibrations.
One beautiful lilac monarch
sings in my ear.

Keep walking.
Love is a blended smoothie
for the soul
that protects the spirit.

I cannot resist the temptation
to reach for a butterfly.
Love whispers in my ear.
You may look and feel

a deep connection,
but you cannot touch the butterfly.
It guards the recipe
of the blended smoothie for soul.

Barefoot

The heartbeat of time caresses my face.
The deep black soil tickles my toes.
I am barefoot against the bull of endurance.
I beat my chest with the urgency of survival.

A swell of self-righteous energy
fills every muscle of my body
with a spiritual flame that burns.

There is no way I will be turned away
from the highway home.
The bear in my chest makes me stride
across the soil toward the heavenly planes.

Ashok K. Bhargava

Ashok K. Bhargava

ASHOK BHARGAVA is a poet, writer, inspirational speaker and a literary consultant. He has attended poetry conferences in Italy, Turkey, India and Philippines. His latest book "Riding the Tide" about his battle with cancer has been translated and published in Arabic, Hindi, Telugu and Bengali languages. He is a contributing writer to several anthologies worldwide including World Poetry Almanac 2014. He has been published in numerous print and online magazines.

Ashok has won many accolades including Poet Ambassador to Japan, Kalidasa International award, World Poetry Lifetime Achievement award, Writers Beyond Borders Peace award and Tapsilog Leadership award for his community involvement. He is founder of Writers International Network Canada Society to discover, nourish, recognize and celebrate writers, poets and artists and to assist them to network with the community at large. He is the author of eight books of poetry and one anthology. He is Artist-in-Residence at Moberly Arts & Cultural Centre and also co-edits the literary section of The Link Newspaper.

Waking Up Dreaming

"… what I did was a spark and it caught on"
~ Claudette Colvin

Think about the days:
the bus, climbing
through backdoor
stay standing
even if the vacant seats
incited you to sit.

You couldn't say a word
when you felt hatred
from the looks,
uncontained.

Think about the days:
the frosty looks and
the cursing voices
made your lungs choked
with every breath.

Then one day you said
enough is enough and
sat down on the vacant seat
stubbornly
with head held high
as they shouted
who's that black lady
on a 'white seat'.

Stepping Out of my Daily Self

I try to see
my Self
in a new spirit
strong and resilient.

But there are so many I's
physical
metaphysical
emotional
egoistic.

Although confused
I know
in the new
season of spring
I will
be a delicate flower
a fresh bloom
to give to the world
my splendor
my fragrance
my seeds
my nectar
my moments of bliss.

Come on
take it all
it is yours.

A Different Dimension

love yourself first
if you want
to love others and
loved by them.

a seed must sprout
a flower must bloom
before a butterfly would
land to taste the nectar.

it is love
that we need
a taste of nectar
to nourish a seed

* This poem approaches the spiritual dimension of human cravings to be loved by friends, relatives, lovers and strangers. Other than the physical experience of being loved, it is the mystic portals of the 'self-realization' which is much more pleasurable than the mundane reality of the universe. It is the ephemerality of everything in life and beyond...

Caroline 'Ceri Naz' Nazareno Gabis

Caroline 'Ceri' Nazareno-Gabis

Caroline 'Ceri Naz' Nazareno-Gabis, author of Velvet Passions of Calibrated Quarks, World Poetry Canada International Director to Philippines is a multi-awarded poet, editor, journalist, educator, peace and women's advocate. She believes that learning other's language and culture is a doorway to wisdom.

Among her poetic belts include **Gabrielle Galloni Memorial Panorama International Youth Award** 2022, Panorama Youth Literary Awards 2020, 7th Prize Winner in the 19th, 20th and 21st Italian Award of Literary Festival; Writers International Network-Canada ''Amazing Poet 2015'', The Frang Bardhi Literary Prize 2014 (Albania), Poet Journalist Award 2014 (Tuzla, Istanbul, Turkey) and World Poetry Empowered Poet 2013 (Vancouver, Canada). She's a featured member of Association of Women's Rights and Development (AWID), The Poetry Posse, Galaktika Poetike, Asia Pacific Writers and Translators (APWT), Axlepino and Anacbanua. Her poetry and children's stories have been featured in different anthologies and magazines worldwide.

Links to her works:

http://panitikan.ph/2018/03/30/caroline-nazareno-gabis/

https://apwriters.org/author/ceri_naz/

http://www.aveviajera.org/nacionesunidasdelasletras/id1181.html

The Moral Courage

Tribute to Claudette Corvin

When you said ' *'I knew then*
and I know now that, when it comes to justice,
stand and say, 'This is not right.''
You are a soujourner of Truth
A woman of substance
Like every passenger's right
Black or white can sit
On the freedom bus,
Wherever you want to;
You've worn your shoes on
With calmness and strong will,
Those days had put heavy pressure
On your chest;
The segregation law had just one eye
But you whipped it,
Because you believed
Civil rights have a place
In every home of Montgomery
In every corner of humanity.
"And You lived to see that change."

mental inertia

sorry is courting the swollen words
with that magic healing touch to the heart
it gives justice, revs up the veins,
the mind could not blackmail the heart
when truth speaks to the soul,
the fragile speaks mouthful of care
and love remains to be love
if all songs be sang to lift swinging moods
to empty anger and disappointments,
those smile carved in your lips
will weep the rivers
from my frozen eyes.

Roundtable of Peace

each and the many
have this heart to share
knowing the purpose,
understanding the reason,
showing the significance,
are life's ensembles;
blaze of cheers
on every face,
come and talk,
walk with peace
one by one,
hand in hand,
side by side
heart to heart
empowering
one another,
inspiring the lips
of compassion
on the humble seat of humanity.

Swapna Behera

Swapna Behera

Swapna Behera is a trilingual poet, translator, environmentalist, editor from India and author of seven books of different genres including one on children's literature on Environment. She is the recipient of International UGADI AWARD 2019, honoured from Gujurat Sahitya Akademi 2022, 2021 International Poesis Award of Honor as Jury, Pentasi B World Fellow Poet, Honoured Poet of India from Seychelles Government and International awards from Algeria, Morocco, Kajhakhstan, modern Arabic Literary Renaissance of Egypt, International Arts Council Argentina etc. Her stories, poems, articles are published in many International and National magazines and ezines. Her poem A NIGHT IN THE REFUGEE CAMP is translated into 67 languages. She has received over 60 National and International Awards. At present she is the Cultural Ambassador for India and South Asia of Inner Child and the life member of Odisha Environmental Society

Email
swapna.behera@gmail.com

Web Site
http://swapnabehera.in/

Claudette Colvin; the civil right activist

She was valiant
cases were filed in the federal court
but who cares?
her brave stand sparked
national attention was drawn
her bravery and determination inspire
she stood for justice and equality
Colvin had no car, she had the examination
a tiny girl reading in a segregated school
a great question mark she put
why at all this colour discrimination?
why at all the black Africans had to leave the seat in public buses
white woman cannot stand
Colvin refused
she protested against injustice
why the black woman can not go to the dress trial room?
history wrote the episode
provoked her to fight for her basic rights
comments in the police stations
abused languages made her strong and stronger
she was the only woman
the pioneer of civil rights movement
at the age of fifteen she was arrested
"Why should I give my seat to a white woman?"
in a crowded bus
a time comes when we have to stand for justice
and say -this is certainly not right
there is no middle way
we can never sugar coat truth, justice and equality
Colvin fought for the constitutional rights
today she is eighty years old

direct or indirect discrimination is harassment
of body, mind and soul
no one is superior than Nature
no one is the policy maker
better than Nature with all colours
that is why she is a difference maker
we salute you dear ……

autobiography of a full stop

my perimeter is an echo
isn't it a silent phoenix?
 a cerulean sky
Is it a song or hymn?
How derogatory to define me
with all intensity and integrity, I allow each comma
as the traffic police allows the ambulance
the world around exists in binaries
you say it is cacophony
some say it is blasphemy
you taste the lemon water of the past
yet have to be ready for the future
I am a full stop
but yes; I am also the rising Sun
beyond any border
that is why my autograph palpitates
and shines in every page of your life's poetry

roti

roti the National Anthem of Democracy
hunger is the tune
food security is the rhythm
roti sings and jumps on the plates
when mother serves with smiles
roti is a full moon
roti is split
 as half-moon on the plate of a mother
as she eats at the last
she serves the other half with love
someday may be to her husband
as he is the father of her children
the other day to her son
when he goes for examination
to her daughter when she goes to her in law's house
roti is the indicator of peace
topics of seminars
roti is prose in poetry
novel or story
essay of a journey
from soil to seed
 seeds to land
land to water
water to germination
crops to harvest
harvest to market
grinding to dough
dough to fire
fire and water entwine to give the shape and size
but behind the stage a team works
marketing, logistics, loans, and tears
at the end of the day

the roti smiles
and why not
it is the boss
of every seminar, every treaty, every currency
every policy and slogan
roti, roti, roti
everywhere roti
it rolls and jumps
with supreme glamour on the ramp
beggar or king
singer or queen
save soil for roti
as roti is a journey
for peace ……...

Albert 'Infinite' Carrasco

Albert “Infinite The Poet” Carrasco is an urban poet, mentor and public speaker.

Albert believes his experience of growing up in poverty, dealing with drugs and witnessing murder over and over were lessons learnt, in order to gain knowledge to teach. Albert’s harsh reality and honesty is a powerfully packed punch delivered through rhyme. Infinite grew up in the east part of the Bronx and still resides there, so he knows many young men will follow the same dark path he followed looking for change. The life of crime should never be an option to being poor but it is, very often.

Infinite poetry @lulu.com

Alcarrasco2 on YouTube

Infinite the poet on reverbnation

Infinite Poetry

http://www.lulu.com/us/en/shop/al-infinite-carrasco/infinite-poetry/paperback/product-21040240.html

Claudette Colvin

I am not the biggest girl, nor am I a bodybuilder but I am black, beautiful and powerful. You're not better than me, I'm not better than you, and for your information I will not bow down to racial intimidation. How dare you. I am only fifteen years old but I know my rights so why am I surrounded by cops with my hands to the back bearing the pain of cuffs being to tight just because I wouldn't give up my seat to a woman that was white. Take the "b" out of "bus" and that's who this vehicle was made for… us. Like I said I know my rights and I am no criminal, I am in intelligent girl that happens to be part of the NAACP youth council in Booker T. Washington high school in Montgomery. Luckily that day I was on the bus with another strong black woman, Ruth Hamilton. The bus driver Robert W Cleere asked both of us to give up our seats and move to the rear for white folk, we both refused, our stance was clear. A black man gave up his seat for Mrs. Hamilton, I refused to move and was forcibly removed by police men Thomas J. Ward and Paul Headley, this event happened nine months before Rosa Parks was arrested, my mentor and the NAACP secretary.

Painted pictures

When I paint pictures with urban scriptures it's a verbal moma exhibition in cerebellums, infinite is the poetic equivalent to Basquiat, ghetto life expressionism. experience is the color that drips from the brush i clutch, when it touches canvas, sunshine and rain, joy and pain mix to create a beautifully ugly masterpiece to embed in my readers and listeners' brains. I started from the bottom of the pot like coke and soda before the water, rose to the top in the pyrex hierarchy because i'm hard like when the process is over. i had to be in order to deal with all the hurt from leaves that fell from the family tree into cemeteries while trying to end poverty. life went from welfare to wealthy to the graveyard quickly. so many died young in the slums, where i'm from at twenty two you're considered a senior because most don't make it to see twenty one. None of my homies got a chance to die of a natural cause, I had hope when it was body shots, then relied on faith when i saw heads wrapped in gauze.

Amnio

Soon after the leaking of amnio premature infinite took his first breaths out the abdomen, i didn't have to wait till experience drama from hell on earth because i was birthed thru a traumatic c section.

Doc put me in the incubator but i didn't need a scully or socks on my feet because moms sun was born with heat, went from the hospital straight to the school of hard knocks to start earning my doctrine of the streets.

I started overstanding my forte of poetry early, my first eleven years of life was beautiful then in the blink
of an eye beauty turned ugly. pop duke lost a battle with the reaper, he was the breadwinner, without him we had to wait till the first for breakfast lunch and diner.

Growing up i felt as if i already had the world in my hands, by twelve it was no longer the world but the "girl" in my hands, poverty changed plans, I am a son of a hustler so it was easy to get my hands on grams.

I was considered a crack baby, the streets spoon fed me thinkn i wasn't ready, but they saw how i got rid of packs quickly daily, morning to night i was out there steady, so them zips with jacks went to weight and frequent trips to smoke shops coppn bottles and caps.

I went from shaking cereal boxes to make sure i didn't digest a roach to upscale restaurants poppn champagne toast after toast, from walking these New York streets to cruise control on highways so i can roll as i coast.

The streets let me taste success, it was just the calm before the storm, then the process of death and three days of rain became the norm where everyone is still hustling and waiting to see who dies next.

Death wasn't a deterrent we all stood on the block and prayed to defy the odds, now i stare at marble rock with the names or faces of all those that returned to god

Michelle
Joan
Barulich

Michelle Joan Barulich

Michelle Joan Barulich was born in Honolulu, Hawaii on the island of Oahu. She started writing poetry and songs with her younger brother Paul. They have written many songs in their teen years. She is currently studying Alternative Medicine and would like to become a Homeopathic Doctor. Michelle loves all kinds of animals and birds; she does wild rehabilitation. She has also rescued rock pigeons that make great pets.

https://www.facebook.com/michelle.barulich

Brave Soul

Claudette your bravery astounds me.
At the tender age of only fifteen
to stand up against authority
without a flinch
You must have a spirit of a warrior.
while maintaining control
I hope humanity can grow
with love and kindness
Your legacy lives on..

Iconoslast

From the words of a broken heart
I have to say
I haven't seen the light for a day
I do not want to anyway
It won't ever agree with me
But I will try to
Between the nights
I have to agree even so
The night is tied

Look around you
What do you see
Stars are falling in and out of time
It's a journey to no man's land
Back to reality, breaker of illusions
I have to say
People are always saying things they shouldn't say
Put it away
Hide it away
and don't show it anyways

But judging just wouldn't be right
It's like mixing day into night
Thinking of love and money at times
Can bring your mind into a raceless fight

Maybe my light right now is at a low key
Or maybe it's just a case of my dark depression
Someday, it will be over and done
..And I haven't seen the light
For a day
I do not want to anyway
It won't ever agree with me ever again
But I will try to.....

Ring In

Ring in, ring out
Ring in, one comes in
One leaves the world
One feels the cold
One strikes the gold

Ring in, two just started there journey
Two just decided to go there own way
Two dreams about there plan
Two dreamers crash into the light

Ring in, three little kids play on the street
Three little kids get hit in the crossfire
Hear the silver bells ring

To celebrate;
or to mourn;

Hear the glasses cling
As they hold them up

Ring in,
Ring out...

Eliza Segiet

Eliza Segiet

Eliza Segiet graduated with a Master's Degree in Philosophy at Jagiellonian University.
Received *Global Literature Guardian Award* – from Motivational Strips, World Nations

Writers' Union and Union Hispanomundial De Escritores (UHE) 2018.

Nominated for the Pushcart Prize 2019, 2021.

Laureate *Naji Naaman Literary Prize 2020*, *International Award Paragon of Hope* (2020),

World Award 2020 *Cesar Vallejo* for Literary Excellence.

Laureate of the Special Jury *Sahitto International Award* 2021, World Award *Premiul Fănuș Neagu* 2021.

Finalist *Golden Aster Book* World Literary Prize 2020, *Mili Dueli* 2022, Voci nel deserto 2022.

At the international Festival of Poetry CAMPIONATO MONDIALE DI POESIA (2021/2022) she won the title of vice-champion of the world.

Award BHARAT RATNA RABINDRANATH TAGORE INTERNATIONAL AWARD (2022).

The White Section

For . . . Claudette Colvin

From behind the curtain of silence,
she began calling for equality.

Suddenly, she found enough strength
in her not to get up.
She did not vacate her seat
in the *white part* of the bus.

Should she have been sitting
in the colored-people section?
Of course, she should!

Not giving up the forbidden seat
was her manifesto
against segregation!

She probably knew
that it is not the color of one's eyes
or skin
that defines one's humanity.

Translated by Dorota Stępińska

Illusion

Crumbled time in-between
real and unreal
and yet alive,
drilling a dry illusion of the intangible.

It's hard to leave the state,
in which
a delusion of truth orders to stay.
To be there where it's better,
though the world of own,
not always colorful thoughts,
is right there.

The drilled encircling space hurts,
an inside affords other hues,
not sensed by everyone,
but those, who
– perhaps –
experience fuller.

Translated by Ula de B.

Ostensible Treasures

Everything connects them. Always together.
Slow they come to terms with passing away.
They know,
the inevitability of the end
will touch everyone.

Tied to life,
they still don't want to part
the ostensible treasures from the past.

They understood,
that they were merely so that,
their open house
wiles the guests to its thresholds.

The facade building,
the imitated friends
– that was the truth.
Only what was left of it?

The time leveled the reality
– alone,
tied to one another
they don't reminisce over the past.

Translated by Ula de B.

William S. Peters Sr.

Bill's writing career spans a period of over 50 years. Being first Published in 1972, Bill has since went on to Author in excess of 50 additional Volumes of Poetry, Short Stories, etc., expressing his thoughts on matters of the Heart, Spirit, Consciousness and Humanity. His primary focus is that of Love, Peace and Understanding!

Bill says . . .

I have always likened Life to that of a Garden. So, for me, Life is simply about the Seeds we Sow and Nourish. All things we "Think and Do", will "Be" Cause and eventually manifest itself to being an "Effect" within our own personal "Existences" and "Experiences" . . . whether it be Fruit, Flowers, Weeds or Barren Landscapes! Bill highly regards the Fruits of his Labor and wishes that everyone would thus go on to plant "Lovely" Seeds on "Good Ground" in their own Gardens of Life!

to connect with Bill, he is all things Inner Child

www.iaminnerchild.com

Personal Web Site

www.iamjustbill.com

Claudia

Did I inspire Rosa . . . doesn't matter,
For we were all too damn tired
To give up our seats on the bus
Which we too paid to ride . . .
All because you are . . . ?
And I am NOT!!!!

Some times it is the small things . . .
Some times it is the big things,
Or the timing of day or night, but in the end,
Are you willing to
Stand up / sit down / take a knee / fight
For what is right

And a child shall lead them . . .

Thank you Claudia

Spring is Sprung

I could smell it in the air,
The fragrance of the
Glorious approaching Spring.

We the children
Shall dance in celebration
Once again
To the music of
The budding,
The blossoming and blooming
Of the flowers
And their vibrancy of light
That color our world
With the promise
Of a sweet harvest.

No more bitter cutting cold winds
To slice to the 'quick'
Of our souls,
Or our temperance

The rains shall visit upon us
To softly, surely rinse away
The past season's angst
That which was made
Of semi-sedantary things

Remember, as
We sat by the fires,
Telling stories
Drinking our Chai
Sharing tales of past times

While our eyes twinkle with a wonder
For the coming spring
Our warm beds and blankets,
Soft pillows
And shortened days
Embraced us
Fed our expectations and dreams
As we imagine once again
Our spirits running nakedly
Through the fields,

Or take a sauntering stroll
Through the gardens
That ardently call
For our holy presence ...
Come, come my child,
Come, and visit with us
For 'Spring is Sprung'
And soon come
The nectar
And the gatherers,
The bees and butterflies
Who shall feed us all.

'Spring is Sprung'

Pain

She had a heart
That rivaled her imagination..
She somehow found a way
To believe
In most men
She took time to know ...
They all were named
Prince Charming

Many of the stories
They inscribed upon her heart
Did not go the way
She would have thought ....
Sure, she kissed a few frogs,
And others after a time
Turned into frogs and dragons and snakes,
Exposing their true slimy
Reptilian character

Her heart by default
Was trusting,
But who amongst us wishes
To experience
A hard hearted life?
.....
Thus the pain was inevitable,
A small price to pay
For those
Gloriously euphoric moments
When love was all she saw,

And filled her heart
With expectations of
What was to come next.
.... Pain

Somewhere in the deep recesses of her truth,
She knew what awaited her on the path of 'Love's' pursuit,
But she traveled anyway even for the brief sojourn, for she never lost her hope.

The Butterfly Effect

"IS" in effect

William S. Peters, Sr.

April

2023

Featured Poets

Maxwanette A Poetess

Alonzo Gross

Türkan Ergör

Ibrahim Honjo

I
Fly
because
I Can
. . . said the Dreamer to the world.
www.iamjustbill.com

Maxwanette
A
Poetess

Maxine A. Moncrieffe aka Maxwanette A Poetess born to Jamaican parents. She is a published Poet, Author, Self-Publisher with Amazon KDP, Writer, Business Owner; "P.L.O.T.S.~Proofing & Promoting Services, LLC," and dba "Cyber Clerical Associates, LLC," Owner / Founder / Editor-in-chief of "P.L.O.T.S. - Creatives Magazine," Notary Public (FL & GA), podcast host on Anchor & Spotify w/P.L.O.T.S. - Podcast, and operates the Facebook group "P.L.O.T.S. - Creatives Bridge." She created P.L.O.T.S - Poetry, Language Of The Soul, to unite & assist Poets & Creatives across the globe.

It Goes On

It was eerily quiet.
The thumping of my heart,
ached the sides of my Soul.

Movements were forgotten,
as the flow of life,
came to a stagnating crawl.

The shallowness of breath,
beckoned to death, to take hold.
For the will to live was lost in tears.

Flickering flashbacks of laughter & joy,
floated around remnants of gifts.
Reminders of the ghostlike connection.

Gone was the woe & sorrow,
of love lost.
Embracing the fullness & warmth of life...

It goes on.

She Was

She was shy.
She didn't know why.
At her worst moment,
she even had forgotten how to cry.

She was humbled & lacking of judgment.
For she had made her own mistakes,
burnt her own bridges, birthed her seeds,
within her own chaos, of mental & physical anguish.

She was scorned.
She had thought she had forgotten her self-worth,
until she learned that she was raped, robbed, and denied its existence.

She was lost.
Like a plastic bag, caught in a whirlwind of;
highs, lows, wherever the wind blows.
Without knowledge of herself, she was battered from pillar to post.

She was reflective.
As life showed her the reality of pains,
that she was clueless as how to fix.
The repeated chaotic footsteps, as her bones & soul ached with each movement.

But always deep inside,
She knew.
There was a bud, damaged, warped, & timid.
As life wondered how it grew.

She was scared.
Taken aback by the power of her words.
Yet drawn with a yearning,
To the sound of her own voice, coded with a path of continuous knowledge.

She was enlightened.
For she finally figured out the missing pieces;
as she realigned, changed, shifted, ironed out, repaired, healed, forgave, loved, shared, became...

She was life.
She was death...
Yet, with each breath, she was...

A Gift (Haiku)

Love can be the change

It is a gift we all have

It is possible

Alonzo Gross

Alonzo Gross

zO-AlonzO Gross is an American Rap Artist, Composer, Producer Actor, Dancer, Writer, Publisher, Author & Multi Award Winning Poet. He is the Author of :
Inspiration, Harmony & The World Within (2012)
Soul Elixir: The WritingZ of zO (2018)
POEMZ 4 U AND YOURZ (2021)
The Visions of Beya Bean Blue
(2023) (Children's book)
the mc (The Meditative ContemplationZ) 2023 and
The Seed Royale Anthology Compilation book 1
(Executive producer & Contributor).
zO lives in Pennsylvania with his Wife and 3 children.

Betcha know now...

Betcha know now ~•
Ain't no way no how ~•
that I would letcha so foul ~•
go astray then
throw in towel ~•

Betcha know now °
why u never (really)
could smile
still made it just about "U"
then severed
the rest of the vows °

Betcha know now `
I won't fagetcha stole
but now `
I figured U'd regretcha stole
but Wow `
U quickta fagetcha stole
& Now `

I Betcha know why ^
Thy Ole' Karma letZ U cry ^

Heart O' coal
Infectious scowl ()
But yep...
I Betcha know Now ()
zO

Fear of Horses...

I used 2 be afraid
Of the light
from the Sun -)(

Used 2 be afraid
Of the flight
from the Jay birdZ
that sung-)(

I used 2 be afraid
Of the night
so I would shun-)(
the fight
But really
twas I Afraid
of what I might become -)(

The sum of my losses ~
ThatZ when
I wouldst hold the drum
Know the Sun
Then Overcome
My Fear of Horses. ~

(©onclusion)

Anywhere
(Near Horses)...(haiku)

AND when Itz the End/
May i Run with the Horses
Being Free as Them/.

Caligula's last stand...

Somewhere,
betwixt the misty caveZ •
of mine conscience,
where some wouldst stare \
pondering the once
glitzy dayZ •
those putrid timeZ
Wherein I wast lead bare \
by mine own divine mind
of dew drifted nonsense

twas I whomest eerily chased
the ether's face
Dearly `
in the form
of the graveZ •
I duly wouldst embrace
so effortlessly
Sincerely `

Yes I,
The Faithful Faithless ~
burning,
in a Cauldron O' secretZ
yearning 4 a discerning
2 seeith the sea's crest
death I,
felt thy breath yet
mine care hath becomest
numb, morbidly
shapeless ~

tasting life's unhinged sour
in the sweetness ()
tho mine pride wouldst rather lie
thence repeat this ()
still I doth cringe in this hour
complete in mine incompleteness ()

But I tell u this
tis' the loneliest `
whomest Art the most sanctimonious `
In their self ®ighteous
LiveZ
their pompas subversion °
with their wealth living lifeless
In an attempt 2 flee their internal
LieZ
through Nocturnal excursionZ °
running in the
cunning night's lust...

Ashamed \
in their
egregiousness *
A lame \
Wherefore repenting
with a tongue in cheek
facetiousness *
All the same \

But Nay,
I nev'r doth ©rieth aloud
In mine aching neurosis {°}
A self deprecation
Embracing of an enabling
Justification

an unjust vocation
A most altrocius {°}
disabling psychosis {°}

(Drinkin' from mine own chalice
O' dethroned divine Malice)

Mine Heart beating
but twas I with deaf eyeZ
And blind earZ
refuseth ta listen °
feeling abused
Wherefore doth I
Retreat,
from mine mission °
Unloosed
from thy sweet noose
Unamused
leaving thy prison °
Like some fleeting apparition °

too proud ta
stand up
And cry
Wherefore,
I sit me down
2 Verily sigh

In some vacant street lot _
this is grown folk talk
I kid ye not _
but when my cousin's
body dropped _

Mine tearZ burned /

whilst at the lectern /
coulda sworn her neck turned /
Death ain't alwayZ
respect earned /

(No goalZ in thy tournament
Only SoulZ in skieZ firmament)

Nevertheless...

that spring
I smelled the coming doom *
the death sting
Sumthin' bout
the Summer's Moon *
brought on the beast
Whomest bled thingZ

Against the fickle forces ^
Burying desire,
tarrying in the mire
Carryin'g the wayward weight
Of guiltZ heavy loses ^

But Shouldst ye death
Carry ye away,
2 thy discernment's treasure ()()
where it shalt remain
as mud In hallowed plain
void of armZ
which canst not measure ()()
A woe in thy charitable almZ

Hurt in my duplicity ~
Still searchin' 4 my tis' of thee ~

No Church in my vicinity ~
threw dirt pon' mine will's
divinity ~
The palmZ of fate,
real Haunting Me
Wherefore
taketh what ye~
want from me ~
taketh pain
ev'r strong in thee ~
taketh rainZ
the weathered stormZ
ye flee ~
But nay,
taketh not
mine song from me. ~

Türkan Ergör

Türkan Ergör

Türkan Ergör, Sociologist, Philosopher, Writer, Poet, Ambassador for Peace.

Türkan Ergör was born in 19 March 1975 in city Çanakkale, Turkey. She is from city İzmir, Turkey. Her father name is Sait Halim Ergör.

She was selected International "Best Poet 2020". She was selected International "Best Poet, Author / Writer 2021". She was selected International "Best Poet, Writer / Author 2022".

Türkan Ergör was given the title of Princess.

Forget

Forget
It is to exterminate darkness, pain
It is to erase past, memories
It is to tear old pages
It is to write the book from afresh
Forget
It is end of the lie
It is the beginning of truth
Forget
It is closing of the past
It is the beginning of the future
And
Forget
It is to live from the beginning
Hopes
Memories.

There Is Journey

If him is going
Him had to go
If him is not returning
Him had to stay
This road has an end
There is journey at the end of this road
There is leave
There is eternity
Every human
As like every passenger
One day depart
Him completes his own life.

If I Could Return

Everyone finally returns
Goes where they belongs
Maybe they want to go
Maybe they don't want to go
But
Finally
People returns
To where they belong
Their becomes request to return
Perhaps unintentionally
Reluctantly
But l
I would want to return
If l could return
Where l belong
Quietly
Because I saw a rose
Never seen before
In the feelings garden.

Ibrahim Honjo

Ibrahim Honjo

Ibrahim Honjo is a Canadian poet-writer, who writes in Bosnian, and English language. He has worked as an economist, journalist, editor, marketing director, and property manager. He is currently retired and resides in Vancouver, BC.

Honjo is author 24 published books in Serbo-Croatian Language, (10 books in English, 3 books bilingually (in English and Serbo-Croatian language). In addition, 4 joints' books of poems published with Serbian poets. His poems have been represented in more than 50 world anthologies.

Some of Honjo's poems have been translated in 17 languages. He received several prizes for his poetry.

Harmony Or Illusion

I never doubted God's power
because I never met God
between us, there was always a gap
deep and wide like an ocean

I doubt the truth
I don't trust people
and their tendency to believe in God
it is all a pure masquerade
it is all about money
all it came to be in fashion
and fad

I never knelt before anyone
even when I was afraid of myself
I believed in the word and its power
I lied to myself
that I mastered the game of words

my childhood misconceptions about people
were deleted by my experience

I stopped trusting a man's word
a promise is a comfort for a fool
I am not in that story
madness comes at the end

my trip to the magic
offers a new disharmony of nature

all beauty is woven in the eyes of a woman
from a woman’s eyes I draw my inner harmony
and illusions

I'm staying...

In vino veritas???

Trinity

I was born on a stone
under that star
below which it does not grow
poisonous plants

poison has always been brought
from the west and the east
it sits below the star
under which it easily succeeded
and hated greed

by ethnicity, I am a Man
my nationality is Earthen
and faith Love

I live and I do not leave a trace
which other people will follow
everybody has traces that blindly follow

It is my right and my duty
to not stop from my way
and to get back under the rock
under that star
below which no poison is growing up

only words will remain behind me
Man, Earthen, Love
as a sacred trinity
conceived
withered and died with me
and in me

This Morning

This morning
a bird landed
on the window of my poem
in the form of a letter
unseen so far

she carried me
and my word
in her chirping

I don't know
whether
because of this
the morning cried

Remembering

our fallen soldiers of verse

Janet Perkins Caldwell

February 14, 1959 ~ September 20, 2016

Alan W. Jankowski

16 March 1961 ~ 10 March 2017

Inner Child Press

News

Poetry Posse Members

We are so excited to share and announce a few of the current books, as well as the new and upcoming books of some of our Poetry Posse authors.

On the following pages we present to you ...

Alicja Maria Kuberska

Jackie Davis Allen

Gail Weston Shazor

hülya n. yılmaz

Nizar Sartawi

Elizabeth E. Castillo

Faleeha Hassan

Fahredin Shehu

Kimberly Burnham

Caroline 'Ceri' Nazareno

Eliza Segiet

Teresa E. Gallion

William S. Peters, Sr.

Now Available

www.innerchildpress.com

Now Available

www.innerchildpress.com

Pulling Coats
Shareef Abdur-Rasheed

Now Available

www.innerchildpress.com

Now Available

www.innerchildpress.com

Fahredin Shehu
ORMUS

Now Available

www.innerchildpress.com

Now Available

www.innerchildpress.com

Now Available at

www.amazon.com/gp/product/B08MYL5B7S/ref=dbs_a_def_rwt_hsch_vapi_tkin_p1_i2

Now Available at

www.innerchildpress.com

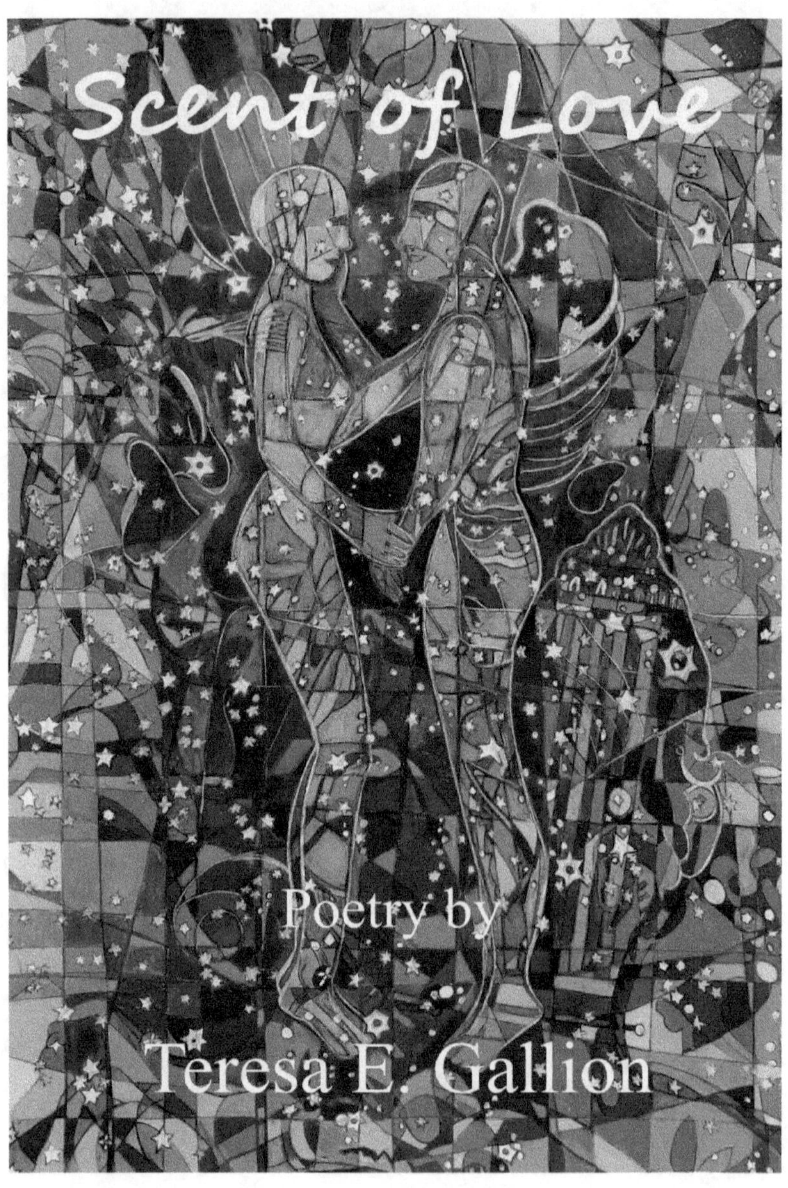

Now Available

www.innerchildpress.com

Now Available

www.innerchildpress.com

Now Available

www.innerchildpress.com

Now Available

www.innerchildpress.com

COMING SOON

www.innerchildpress.com

The Book of krisar

volume v

william s. peters, sr.

Now Available

www.innerchildpress.com

The Book of krisar

The Book of krisar

william s. peters, sr.

Now Available

www.innerchildpress.com

Now Available

www.innerchildpress.com

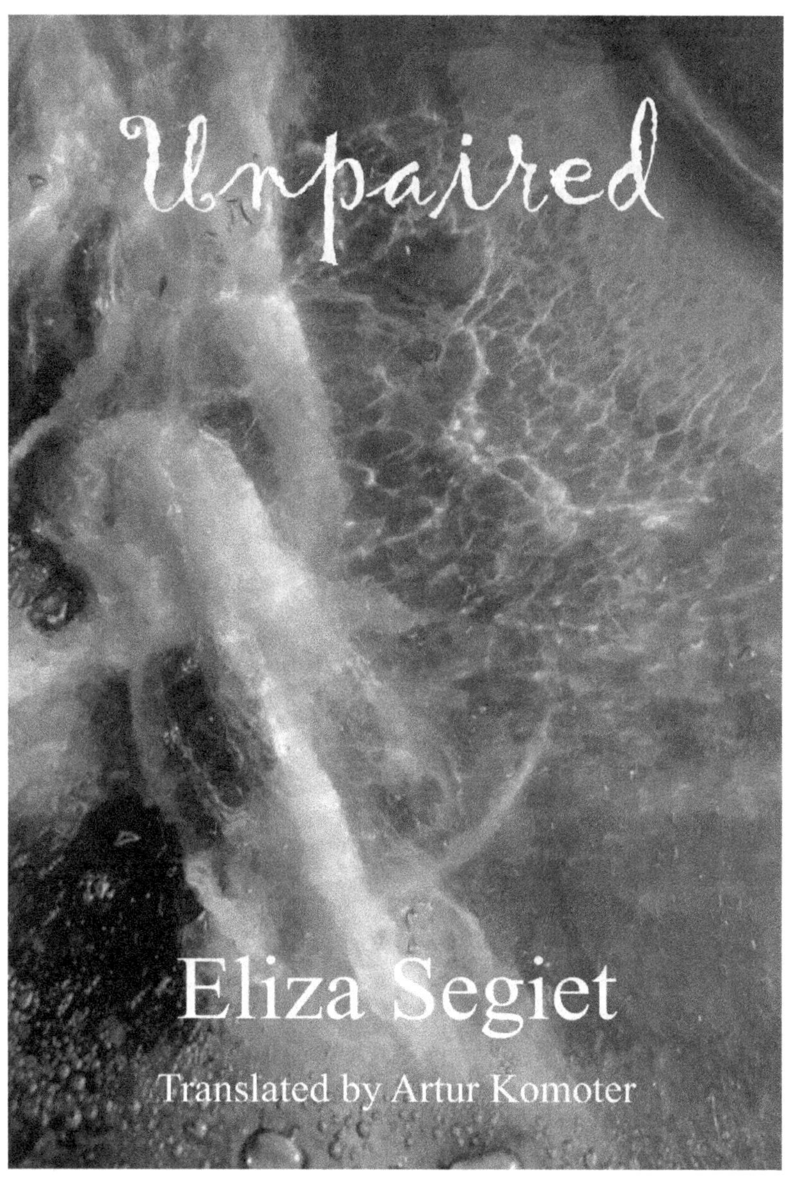

Private Issue

www.innerchildpress.com

Now Available

www.innerchildpress.com

Now Available at

www.innerchildpress.com

Now Available at

www.innerchildpress.com

Now Available at

www.innerchildpress.com

Now Available at

www.innerchildpress.com

Now Available at

www.innerchildpress.com

Now Available at

www.innerchildpress.com

Now Available at

www.innerchildpress.com

Now Available at

www.innerchildpress.com

Now Available at

www.innerchildpress.com

Now Available at

www.innerchildpress.com

Breakfast

for

Butterflies

Faleeha Hassan

Now Available at

www.innerchildpress.com

Now Available at

www.innerchildpress.com

Now Available at

www.innerchildpress.com

Now Available at

www.innerchildpress.com

Other

Anthological

works from

Inner Child Press International

www.innerchildpress.com

Now Available

www.worldhealingworldpeacepoetry.com

Now Available

www.worldhealingworldpeacepoetry.com

Now Available

www.innerchildpress.com

the Heart of a Poet
words for a better tomorrow
The Conscious Poets

Corona
Social Distancing
Poets for Humanity

Poetry
from the
Balkans
The Balkan Poets

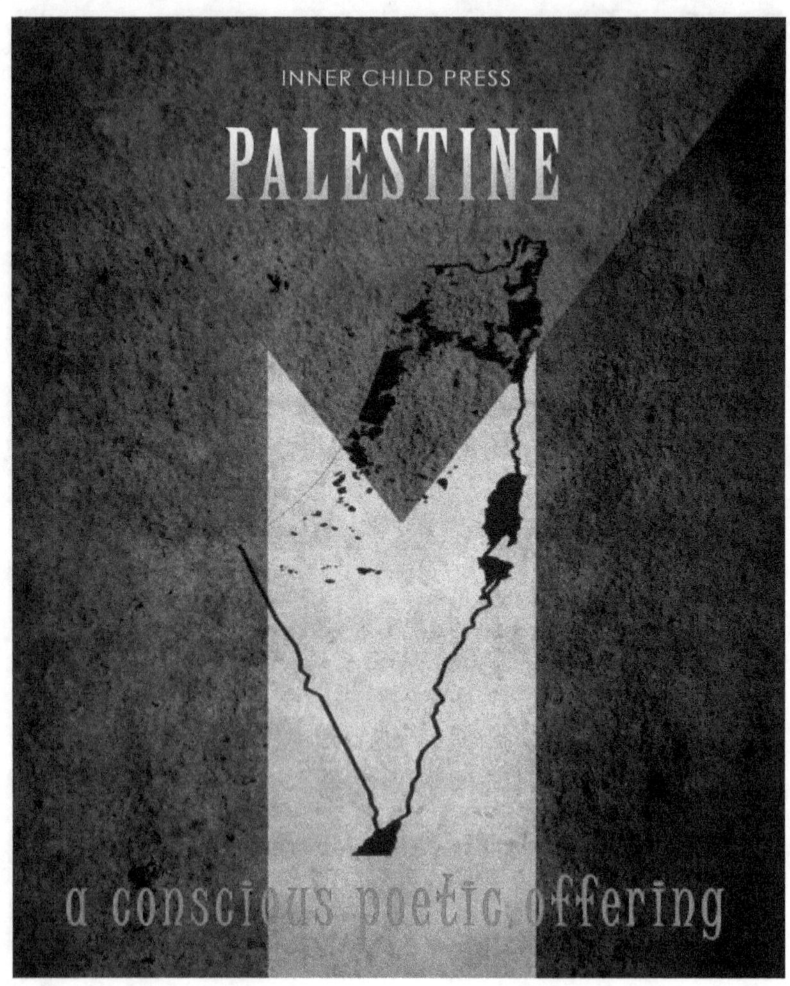

Now Available at

www.innerchildpress.com

Now Available at

www.innerchildpress.com

Now Available

www.worldhealingworldpeacepoetry.com

Now Available

www.worldhealingworldpeacepoetry.com

Now Available

www.worldhealingworldpeacepoetry.com

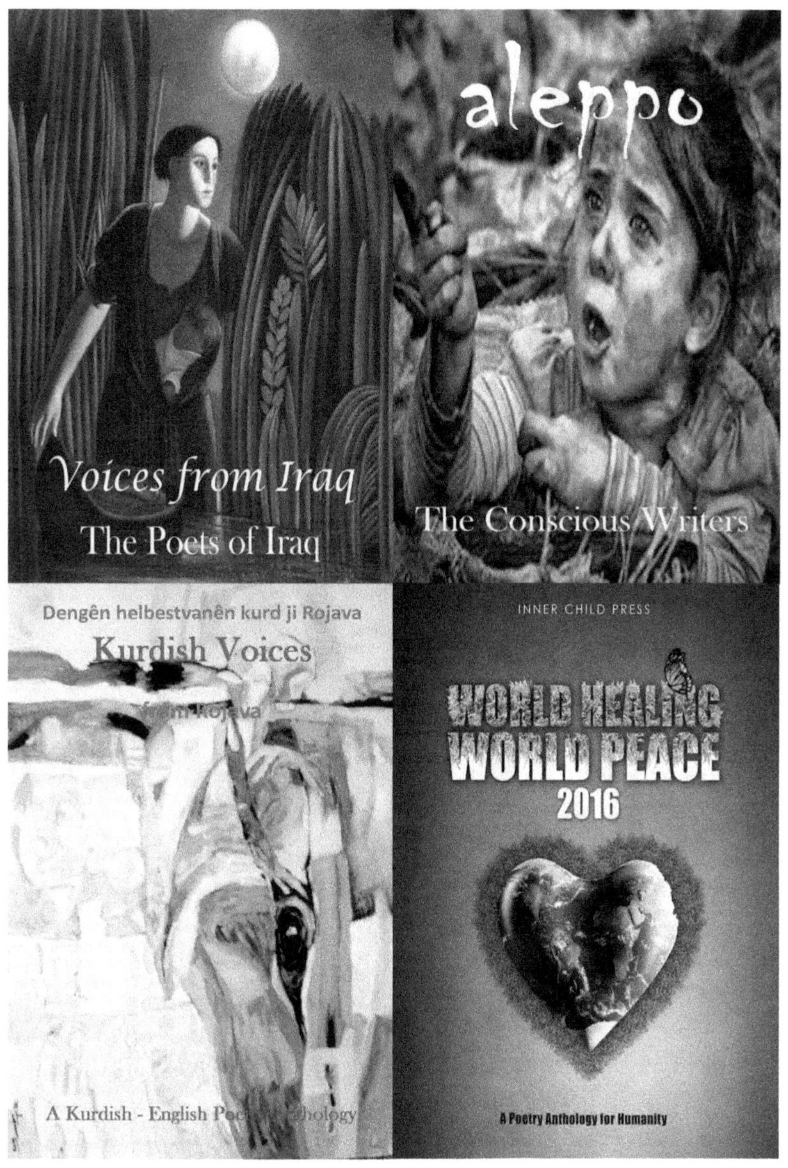

Now Available

www.innerchildpress.com/anthologies

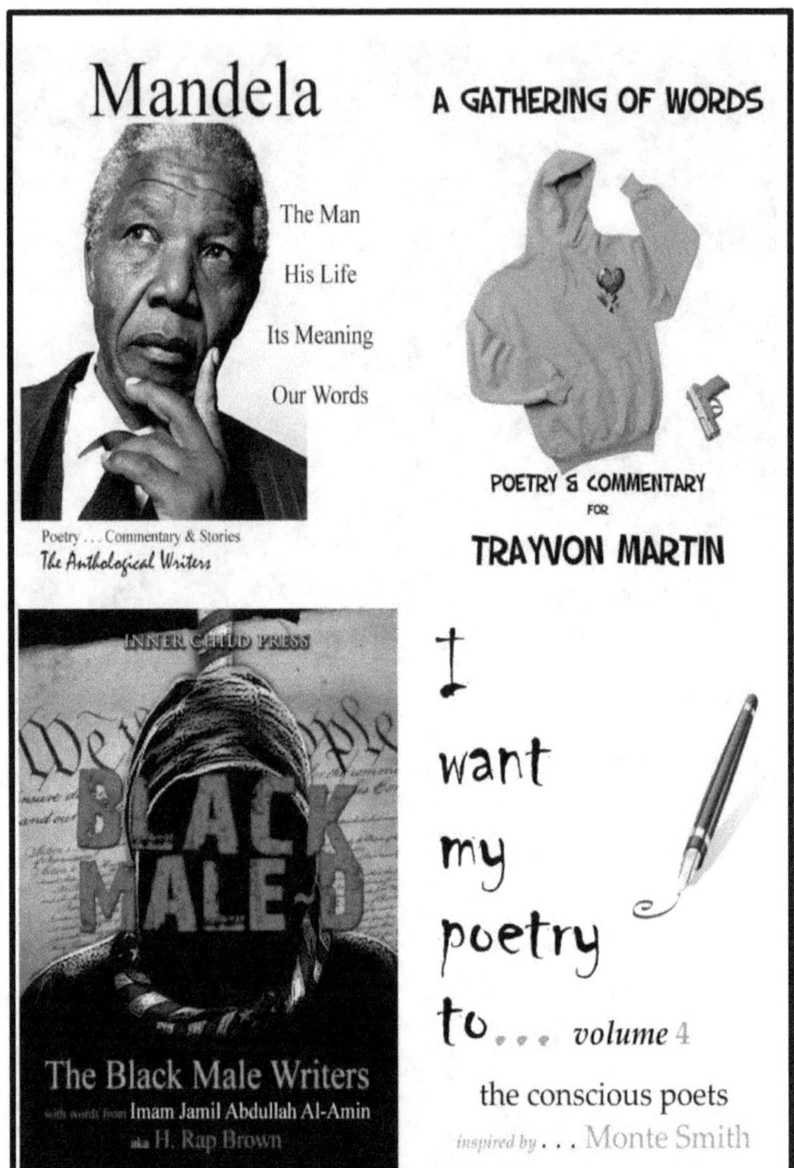

Now Available

www.innerchildpress.com/anthologies

Now Available

www.innerchildpress.com/anthologies

Inner Child Press Anthologies

a
Poetically
Spoken
Anthology
volume I
Collector's Edition

Now Available

www.innerchildpress.com/anthologies

Now Available

www.innerchildpress.com/anthologies

Inner Child Press Anthologies

Now Available

www.innerchildpress.com/the-year-of-the-poet

Inner Child Press Anthologies

Now Available

www.innerchildpress.com/the-year-of-the-poet

Inner Child Press Anthologies

The Year of the Poet

September 2014

September Feature Poets

Florence Malone * Keith Alan Hamilton

The Poetry Posse

Jamie Bond * Gail Weston Shazor * Albert 'Infinite' Carrasco * Siddartha Beth Pierce
Janet P. Caldwell * June 'Bugg' Barefield * Debbie M. Allen * Tony Henninger
Joe DaVerbal Minddancer * Robert Gibbons * Neetu Wali * Shareef Abdur-Rasheed
Kimberly Burnham * William S. Peters, Sr.

THE YEAR OF THE POET

October 2014

The Poetry Posse

Jamie Bond * Gail Weston Shazor * Albert 'Infinite' Carrasco * Siddartha Beth Pierce
Janet P. Caldwell * June 'Bugg' Barefield * Debbie M. Allen * Tony Henninger
Joe DaVerbal Minddancer * Robert Gibbons * Neetu Wali * Shareef Abdur-Rasheed
Kimberly Burnham * William S. Peters, Sr.

October Feature Poets

Ceri Naz * Rajendra Padhi * Elizabeth Castillo

Now Available

www.innerchildpress.com/the-year-of-the-poet

THE YEAR OF THE POET II

February 2015

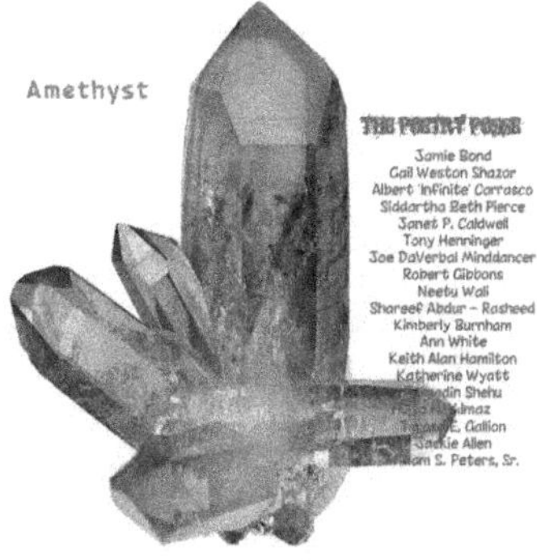

FEBRUARY FEATURE POETS

Iram Fatima * Bob McNeil * Kerstin Centervall

The Year of the Poet II

March 2015

Our Featured Poets

Heung Sook * Anthony Arnold * Alicia Poland

The Poetry Posse 2015

Jamie Bond * Gail Weston Shazor * Albert 'Infinite' Carrasco
Siddartha Beth Pierce * Janet P. Caldwell * Tony Henninger
Joe DaVerbal Minddancer * Neetu Wali * Shareef Abdur – Rasheed
Kimberly Burnham * Ann White * Keith Alan Hamilton
Katherine Wyatt * Fahredin Shehu * Hülya N. Yilmaz
Teresa E. Gallion * Jackie Allen * William S. Peters, Sr.

Now Available

www.innerchildpress.com/the-year-of-the-poet

Inner Child Press Anthologies

The Year of the Poet II

June 2015

June's Featured Poets

Anahit Arustamyan * Yvette D. Murrell * Regina A. Walker

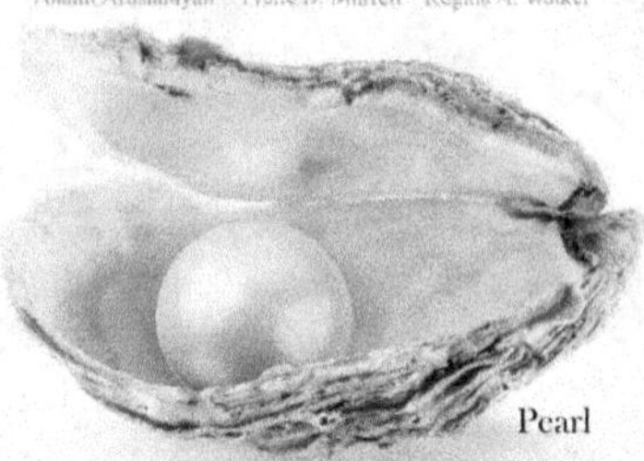

Pearl

The Poetry Posse 2015

Jamie Bond * Gail Weston Shazor * Albert 'Infinite' Carrasco
Siddartha Beth Pierce * Janet P. Caldwell * Tony Henninger
Joe DaVerbal Minddancer * Neetu Wali * Shareef Abdur – Rasheed
Kimberly Burnham * Ann White * Keith Alan Hamilton
Katherine Wyatt * Fahredin Shehu * Hülya N. Yılmaz
Teresa E. Gallion * Jackie Allen * William S. Peters, Sr.

The Year of the Poet II

July 2015

The Featured Poets for July 2015

Abhik Shome * Christina Neal * Robert Neal

Rubies

The Poetry Posse 2015

Jamie Bond * Gail Weston Shazor * Albert 'Infinite' Carrasco
Siddartha Beth Pierce * Janet P. Caldwell * Tony Henninger
Joe DaVerbal Minddancer * Neetu Wali * Shareef Abdur – Rasheed
Kimberly Burnham * Ann White * Keith Alan Hamilton
Katherine Wyatt * Fahredin Shehu * Hülya N. Yılmaz
Teresa E. Gallion * Jackie Allen * William S. Peters, Sr.

The Year of the Poet II

August 2015

Peridot

Featured Poets

Gayle Howell
Ann Chalasz
Christopher Schultz

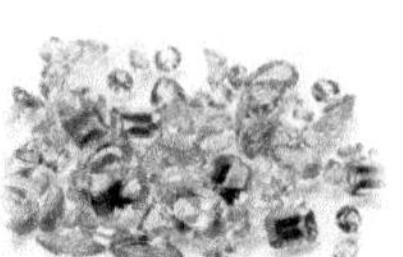

The Poetry Posse 2015

Jamie Bond * Gail Weston Shazor * Albert 'Infinite' Carrasco
Siddartha Beth Pierce * Janet P. Caldwell * Tony Henninger
Joe DaVerbal Minddancer * Neetu Wali * Shareef Abdur – Rasheed
Kimberly Burnham * Ann White * Keith Alan Hamilton
Katherine Wyatt * Fahredin Shehu * Hülya N. Yılmaz
Teresa E. Gallion * Jackie Allen * William S. Peters, Sr.

Now Available

www.innerchildpress.com/the-year-of-the-poet

Now Available

www.innerchildpress.com/the-year-of-the-poet

Inner Child Press Anthologies

Now Available

www.innerchildpress.com/the-year-of-the-poet

Inner Child Press Anthologies

Now Available

www.innerchildpress.com/the-year-of-the-poet

The Year of the Poet IV
January 2017
Jon Winell
Natalie Shields
Quaking Aspen
The Poetry Posse 2017

The Year of the Poet IV
February 2017
Featured Poets
Lin Ross
Witch Hazel
The Poetry Posse 2017

The Year of the Poet IV
March 2017
Featured Poets
Tremell Stevens
Francisca Ricinski
The Eastern Redbud
The Poetry Posse 2017

The Year of the Poet IV
April 2017
Featured Poets
Neptune Barman
The Blossoming Cherry
The Poetry Posse 2017

Inner Child Press Anthologies

The Year of the Poet IV
May 2017

The Flowering Dogwood Tree

Featured Poets
Kallisa Powell
Alicja Maria Kuberska
Fethi Sassi

The Poetry Posse 2017

Gail Weston Shazor * Caroline Nazareno * Bismay Mohanty
Teresa E. Gallion * Anna Jakubczak Vel Ratty Adalon
Joe DaVerbal Minddancer * Shareef Abdur – Rasheed
Albert Carrasco * Kimberly Burnham * Elizabeth Castillo
Hulya N. Yilmaz * Faleeha Hassan * Jackie Davis Allen
Jen Walls * Nizar Sartawi * * William S. Peters, Sr

The Year of the Poet IV
July 2017

Featured Poets
Anca Mihaela Bruma
Ibaa Ismail
Zvonko Taneski

The Oak Moon

The Poetry Posse 2017

The Year of the Poet IV
August 2017

The Poetry Posse 2017

Gail Weston Shazor * Caroline Nazareno *
Teresa E. Gallion * Anna Jakubczak Vel Ratty Adalon
Joe DaVerbal Minddancer * Shareef Abdur – Rasheed
Albert Carrasco * Kimberly Burnham * Elizabeth Castillo
Hulya N. Yilmaz * Faleeha Hassan * Jackie Davis Allen
Jen Walls * Nizar Sartawi * * William S. Peters, Sr.

Now Available

www.innerchildpress.com/the-year-of-the-poet

Inner Child Press Anthologies

Now Available

www.innerchildpress.com/the-year-of-the-poet

Now Available

www.innerchildpress.com/the-year-of-the-poet

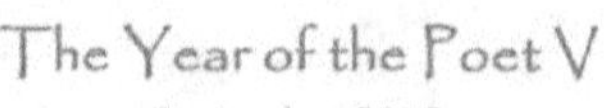

The Year of the Poet V
September 2018

The Aztecs & Incas

Featured Poets

The Poetry Posse 2018

The Year of the Poet V
October 2018

Featured Poets
Alicia Minjarez * Lonneice Weeks-Badley
Lopamudra Mishra * Abdelwahed Souayah

The Poetry Posse 2018
Gail Weston Shazor * Nizar Sartawi * Hülya N. Yılmaz
Jackie Davis Allen * Caroline 'Ceri' Nazareno
Alicja Maria Kuberska * Teresa E. Gallion
Kimberly Burnham * Shareef Abdur – Rasheed
Ashok K. Bhargava * Elizabeth Castillo * Swapna Behera
Tezmin Ition Tsai * William S. Peters, Sr.

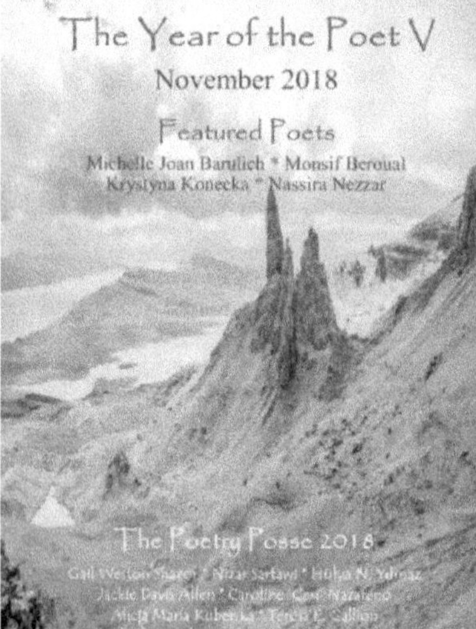

The Year of the Poet V
December 2018

Featured Poets
Rose Terranova Cirigliano
Joanna Kalinowska
Sokolović Emin
Dr. T. Ashok Chakravarthy

The Maori

Gail Weston Shazor * Nizar Sartawi * Hülya N. Yılmaz
Jackie Davis Allen * Caroline 'Ceri' Nazareno
Alicja Maria Kuberska * Teresa E. Gallion
Kimberly Burnham * Shareef Abdur – Rasheed
Ashok K. Bhargava * Elizabeth Castillo * Swapna Behera
Tezmin Ition Tsai * William S. Peters, Sr.

Now Available

www.innerchildpress.com/the-year-of-the-poet

Inner Child Press Anthologies

The Year of the Poet VI
January 2019

Indigenous North Americans

Featured Poets

Houda Elfchtali
Anthony Briscoe
Iram Fatima 'Ashi'
Dr. K. K. Mathew

Dream Catcher

The Poetry Posse 2019

Gail Weston Shazor * Joe Paire * Hülya N. Yilmaz
Jackie Davis Allen * Caroline 'Ceri' Nazareno
Alicja Maria Kuberska * Teresa E. Gallion
Kimberly Burnham * Shareef Abdur – Rasheed
Ashok K. Bhargava * Elizabeth Castillo * Swapna Behera
Tezmin Ition Tsai * William S. Peters, Sr.

The Year of the Poet VI
February 2019

Featured Poets

Marek Lukaszewicz * Bharati Nayak
Aida G. Roque * Jean-Jacques Fournier

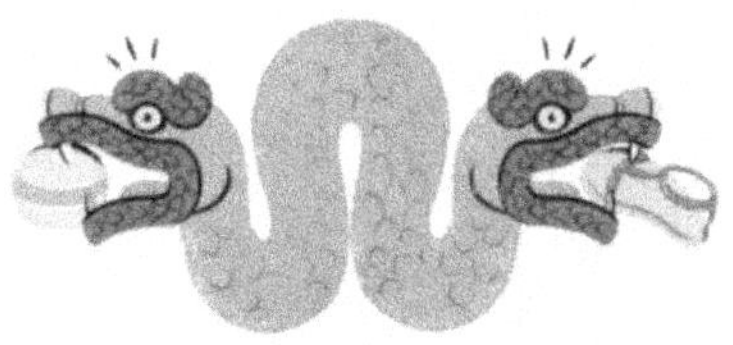

Meso-America

The Poetry Posse 2019

Gail Weston Shazor * Albert Carrasco * Hülya N. Yilmaz
Jackie Davis Allen * Caroline Nazareno * Eliza Segiet
Alicja Maria Kuberska * Teresa E. Gallion * Joe Paire
Kimberly Burnham * Shareef Abdur – Rasheed
Ashok K. Bhargava * Elizabeth Castillo * Swapna Behera
Tezmin Ition Tsai * William S. Peters, Sr.

Now Available

www.innerchildpress.com/the-year-of-the-poet

The Nile Valley

The Poetry Posse 2019

Gail Weston Shazor * Albert Carrasco * Hülya N. Yılmaz
Jackie Davis Allen * Caroline Nazareno * Eliza Segiet
Alicja Maria Kuberska * Teresa E. Gallion * Joe Paire
Kimberly Burnham * Shareef Abdur - Rasheed
Ashok K. Bhargava * Elizabeth Castillo * Swapna Behera
Tzemin Ition Tsai * William S. Peters, Sr.

The Year of the Poet VI

November 2019

Featured Poets

Rozalia Aleksandrova * Orbindu Ganga
Smruti Ranjan Mohanty * Sofia Skleida

Northern Asia

The Poetry Posse 2019

Gail Weston Shazor * Albert Carrasco * Hülya N. Yılmaz
Jackie Davis Allen * Caroline Nazareno * Eliza Segiet
Alicja Maria Kuberska * Teresa E. Gallion * Joe Paire
Kimberly Burnham * Shareef Abdur - Rasheed
Ashok K. Bhargava * Elizabeth Castillo * Swapna Behera
Tzemin Ition Tsai * William S. Peters, Sr.

The Year of the Poet VI

December 2019

Featured Poets

The Poetry Posse 2019

Gail Weston Shazor * Albert Carrasco * Hülya N. Yılmaz
Jackie Davis Allen * Caroline Nazareno * Eliza Segiet
Alicja Maria Kuberska * Teresa E. Gallion * Joe Paire
Kimberly Burnham * Shareef Abdur - Rasheed
Ashok K. Bhargava * Elizabeth Castillo * Swapna Behera
Tzemin Ition Tsai * William S. Peters, Sr.

Now Available

www.innerchildpress.com/the-year-of-the-poet

Now Available

www.innerchildpress.com/the-year-of-the-poet

Now Available

www.innerchildpress.com/the-year-of-the-poet

Now Available

www.innerchildpress.com/the-year-of-the-poet

Inner Child Press Anthologies

The Year of the Poet VIII

May 2021

Featured Global Poets

Paramita Mukherjee Mullick * Rose Zerguine
Jaydeep Sarangi * Bismay Mohanty

Diego Rivera

Poetry . . . Ekphrasticly Speaking

The Poetry Posse 2021

Gail Weston Shazor * Albert Carassco * Hülya N. Yılmaz
Jackie Davis Allen * Caroline Nazareno * Eliza Segiet
Alicja Maria Kuberska * Teresa E. Gallion * Joe Paire
Kimberly Burnham * Shareef Abdur – Rasheed
Ashok K. Bhargava * Elizabeth Castillo * Swapna Behera
Tezmin Ition Tsai * William S. Peters, Sr.

The Year of the Poet VIII

June 2021

Featured Global Poets

Alonzo "zO" Gross * Lali Tsipi Michaeli
Tareq al Karmy * Tirthendu Ganguly

Rayen Kang

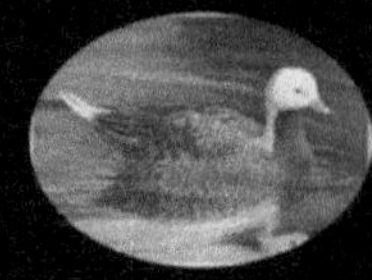

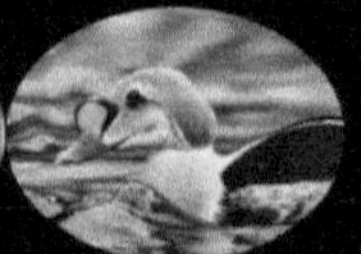

Poetry . . . Ekphrasticly Speaking

The Poetry Posse 2021

Gail Weston Shazor * Albert Carassco * Hülya N. Yılmaz
Jackie Davis Allen * Caroline Nazareno * Eliza Segiet
Alicja Maria Kuberska * Teresa E. Gallion * Joe Paire
Kimberly Burnham * Shareef Abdur – Rasheed
Ashok K. Bhargava * Elizabeth Castillo * Swapna Behera
Tezmin Ition Tsai * William S. Peters, Sr.

The Year of the Poet VIII

July 2021

Featured Global Poets

Iram Jaan * Vesna Mundishevska-Veljanovska
Ngozi Olivia Osuoha * Lan Qyqalla

Goncalao Mabunda

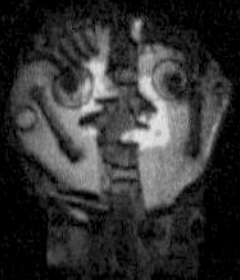

Poetry . . . Ekphrasticly Speaking

The Poetry Posse 2021

Gail Weston Shazor * Albert Carassco * Hülya N. Yılmaz
Jackie Davis Allen * Caroline Nazareno * Eliza Segiet
Alicja Maria Kuberska * Teresa E. Gallion * Joe Paire
Kimberly Burnham * Shareef Abdur – Rasheed
Ashok K. Bhargava * Elizabeth Castillo * Swapna Behera
Tezmin Ition Tsai * William S. Peters, Sr.

The Year of the Poet VIII

August 2021

Featured Global Poets

Caroline Laurent Turunc * Kamal Dhungana
Pankhuri Sinha * Paramita Mukherjee Mullick

Mundara Koorang

Poetry . . . Ekphrasticly Speaking

The Poetry Posse 2021

Gail Weston Shazor * Albert Carassco * Hülya N. Yılmaz
Jackie Davis Allen * Caroline Nazareno * Eliza Segiet
Alicja Maria Kuberska * Teresa E. Gallion * Joe Paire
Kimberly Burnham * Shareef Abdur – Rasheed
Ashok K. Bhargava * Elizabeth Castillo * Swapna Behera
Tezmin Ition Tsai * William S. Peters, Sr.

Now Available

www.innerchildpress.com/the-year-of-the-poet

The Year of the Poet VIII
September 2021
Featured Global Poets
Monsif Beroual * Sandesh Ghimire
Sharmila Poudel * Pavol Janik
Heather Jansch
Poetry . . . Ekphrasticly Speaking
The Poetry Posse 2021
Gail Weston Shazor * Albert Carassco * Hülya N. Yılmaz
Jackie Davis Allen * Caroline Nazareno * Eliza Segiet
Alicja Maria Kuberska * Teresa E. Gallion * Joe Paire
Kimberly Burnham * Shareef Abdur – Rasheed
Ashok K. Bhargava * Elizabeth Castillo * Swapna Behera
Tezmin Ition Tsai * William S. Peters, Sr.
The Year of the Poet VIII
October 2021
Featured Global Poets
C. E. Shy * Saswata Ganguly
Suranjit Gain * Hasiba Hilal
Dale Lamphere
Poetry . . . Ekphrasticly Speaking
The Poetry Posse 2021
Gail Weston Shazor * Albert Carassco * Hülya N. Yılmaz
Jackie Davis Allen * Caroline Nazareno * Eliza Segiet
Alicja Maria Kuberska * Teresa E. Gallion * Joe Paire
Kimberly Burnham * Shareef Abdur – Rasheed
Ashok K. Bhargava * Elizabeth Castillo * Swapna Behera
Tezmin Ition Tsai * William S. Peters, Sr.
The Year of the Poet VIII
November 2021
Featured Global Poets
Errol D. Bean * Ibrahim Honjo
Tanja Ajtic * Rajashree Mohapatra
Andy Goldsworthy
Poetry . . . Ekphrasticly Speaking
The Poetry Posse 2021
Gail Weston Shazor * Albert Carassco * Hülya N. Yılmaz
Jackie Davis Allen * Caroline Nazareno * Eliza Segiet
Alicja Maria Kuberska * Teresa E. Gallion * Joe Paire
Kimberly Burnham * Shareef Abdur – Rasheed
Ashok K. Bhargava * Elizabeth Castillo * Swapna Behera
Tezmin Ition Tsai * William S. Peters, Sr.
The Year of the Poet VIII
December 2021
Featured Global Poets
Orbinda Ganga * Fadairo Tesleem
Anthony Arnold * Iyad Shamasnah
Fredric Edwin Church
Poetry . . . Ekphrasticly Speaking
The Poetry Posse 2021
Gail Weston Shazor * Albert Carassco * Hülya N. Yılmaz
Jackie Davis Allen * Caroline Nazareno * Eliza Segiet
Alicja Maria Kuberska * Teresa E. Gallion * Joe Paire
Kimberly Burnham * Shareef Abdur – Rasheed
Ashok K. Bhargava * Elizabeth Castillo * Swapna Behera
Tezmin Ition Tsai * William S. Peters, Sr.

Inner Child Press Anthologies

The Year of the Poet IX

January 2022

Featured Global Poets

Ratan Ghosh * Christine Neil-Wright
Andrew Scott * Ashok Kumar

Climate Change : The Ice Cap

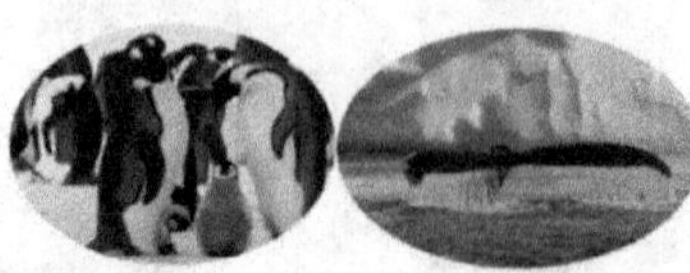

Poetry . . . Ekphrasticly Speaking

The Poetry Posse 2021

Gail Weston Shazor * Albert Carassco * Hülya N. Yılmaz
Jackie Davis Allen * Caroline Nazareno * Eliza Segiet
Alicja Maria Kuberska * Teresa E. Gallion * Joe Paire
Kimberly Burnham * Shareef Abdur – Rasheed
Ashok K. Bhargava * Elizabeth Castillo * Swapna Behera
Tezmin Ition Tsai * William S. Peters, Sr.

The Year of the Poet IX

February 2022

Featured Global Poets

Roza Boyanova * Ramón de Jesús Núñez Duval
Mammad Ismayil * Tarana Turan Rahimli

Climate Change and Mountains

Poetry . . . Ekphrasticly Speaking

The Poetry Posse 2021

Gail Weston Shazor * Albert Carassco * Hülya N. Yılmaz
Jackie Davis Allen * Caroline Nazareno * Eliza Segiet
Alicja Maria Kuberska * Teresa E. Gallion * Joe Paire
Kimberly Burnham * Shareef Abdur – Rasheed
Ashok K. Bhargava * Elizabeth Castillo * Swapna Behera
Tezmin Ition Tsai * William S. Peters, Sr.

The Year of the Poet IX

March 2022

Featured Global Poets

Dimitris P. Kraniotis * Marlene Pasini
Kennedy Ochieng * Swayam Prashant

Climate Change and Space Debris

Poetry . . . Ekphrasticly Speaking

The Poetry Posse 2021

Gail Weston Shazor * Albert Carassco * Hülya N. Yılmaz
Jackie Davis Allen * Caroline Nazareno * Eliza Segiet
Alicja Maria Kuberska * Teresa E. Gallion * Joe Paire
Kimberly Burnham * Shareef Abdur – Rasheed
Ashok K. Bhargava * Elizabeth Castillo * Swapna Behera
Tezmin Ition Tsai * William S. Peters, Sr.

The Year of the Poet IX

April 2022

Featured Global Poets

Alonzo Gross * Dr. Debaprasanna Biswas
Monsif Beroual * Carol Aronoff

Climate Change and Oceans

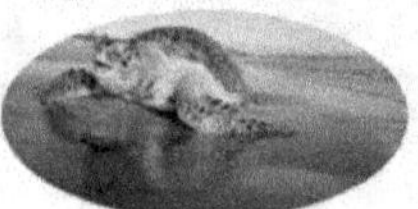

*Celebrating our 100th Edition *

Poetry . . . Ekphrasticly Speaking

The Poetry Posse 2021

Gail Weston Shazor * Albert Carassco * Hülya N. Yılmaz
Jackie Davis Allen * Caroline Nazareno * Eliza Segiet
Alicja Maria Kuberska * Teresa E. Gallion * Joe Paire
Kimberly Burnham * Shareef Abdur – Rasheed
Ashok K. Bhargava * Elizabeth Castillo * Swapna Behera
Tezmin Ition Tsai * William S. Peters, Sr.

Now Available

www.innerchildpress.com/the-year-of-the-poet

Inner Child Press Anthologies

The Year of the Poet IX
September 2022

Featured Global Poets

Ngozi Olivia Osuoha * Biswajit Mishra
Sylwia K. Malinowska * Sajid Hussein

Climate Change and Wind and Weather Patterns

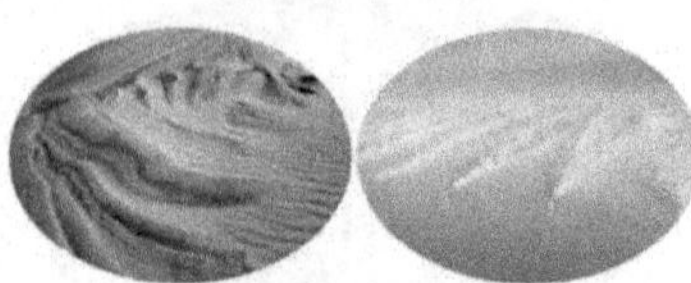

Poetry . . . Ekphrasticly Speaking

The Poetry Posse 2022

Gail Weston Shazor * Albert Carassco * Hülya N. Yilmaz
Jackie Davis Allen * Caroline Nazareno * Eliza Segiet
Alicja Maria Kuberska * Teresa E. Gallion * Joe Paire
Kimberly Burnham * Shareef Abdur – Rasheed
Ashok K. Bhargava * Elizabeth Castillo * Swapna Behera
Tezmin Ition Tsai * William S. Peters, Sr.

The Year of the Poet IX
October 2022

Featured Global Poets

Andrew Kouroupos * Brenda Mohammed
Carthornia Kouroupos * Faleeha Hassan

Climate Change and Oil and Power

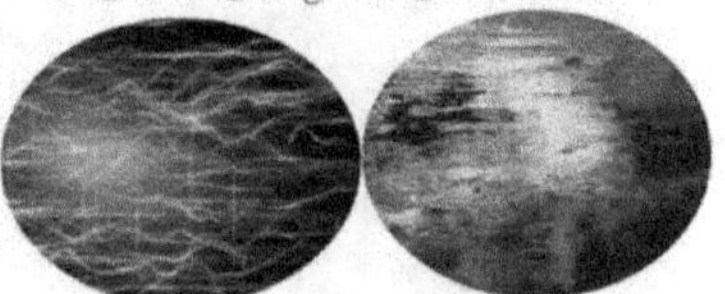

Poetry . . . Ekphrasticly Speaking

The Poetry Posse 2022

Gail Weston Shazor * Albert Carassco * Hülya N. Yilmaz
Jackie Davis Allen * Caroline Nazareno * Eliza Segiet
Alicja Maria Kuberska * Teresa E. Gallion * Joe Paire
Kimberly Burnham * Shareef Abdur – Rasheed
Ashok K. Bhargava * Elizabeth Castillo * Swapna Behera
Tezmin Ition Tsai * William S. Peters, Sr.

The Year of the Poet IX
November 2022

Featured Global Poets

Hema Ravi * Shafkat Aziz Hajam
Selma Kopic * Ibrahim Honjo

Climate Change : Time to Act

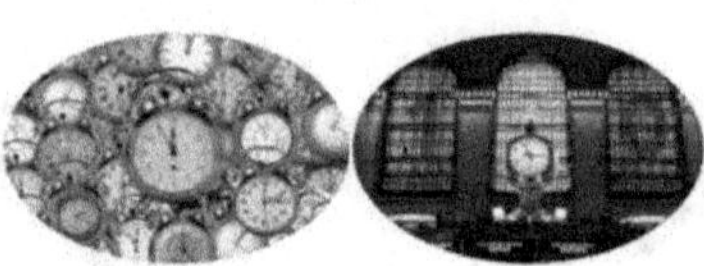

Poetry . . . Ekphrasticly Speaking

The Poetry Posse 2022

Gail Weston Shazor * Albert Carassco * Hülya N. Yilmaz
Jackie Davis Allen * Caroline Nazareno * Eliza Segiet
Alicja Maria Kuberska * Teresa E. Gallion * Joe Paire
Kimberly Burnham * Shareef Abdur – Rasheed
Ashok K. Bhargava * Elizabeth Castillo * Swapna Behera
Tezmin Ition Tsai * William S. Peters, Sr.

The Year of the Poet IX
December 2022

Featured Global Poets

Elarbi Abdelfattah * Lorraine Cragg
Neha Bhandarkar * Robert Gibbons

Climate Change Bees, Butterflies and Insect Life

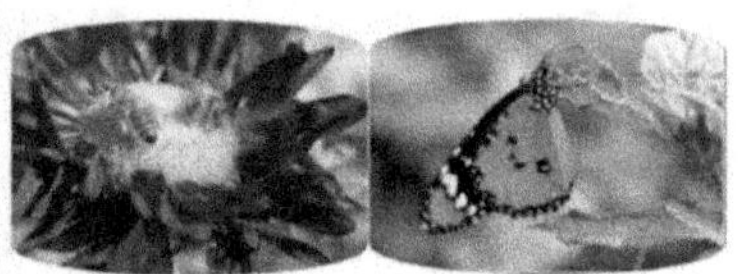

Poetry . . . Ekphrasticly Speaking

The Poetry Posse 2022

Gail Weston Shazor * Albert Carassco * Hülya N. Yilmaz
Jackie Davis Allen * Caroline Nazareno * Eliza Segiet
Alicja Maria Kuberska * Teresa E. Gallion * Joe Paire
Kimberly Burnham * Shareef Abdur – Rasheed
Ashok K. Bhargava * Elizabeth Castillo * Swapna Behera
Tezmin Ition Tsai * William S. Peters, Sr.

Now Available

www.innerchildpress.com/the-year-of-the-poet

The Year of the Poet X

January 2023

Featured Global Poets

JuNe Barefield * Swayam Prashant
Willow Rose * Shabbirhusein K Jamnagerwalla

Children: Difference Makers

Iqbal Masih

The Poetry Posse 2023

Gail Weston Shazor * Albert Carassco * Hülya N. Yılmaz
Jackie Davis Allen * Caroline Nazareno * Kimberly Burnham
Alicja Maria Kuberska * Teresa E. Gallion * Joe Paire
Michelle Joan Barulich * Shareef Abdur – Rasheed
Ashok K. Bhargava * Elizabeth Castillo * Swapna Behera
Tezmin Ition Tsai * Eliza Segiet * William S. Peters, Sr.

Now Available

www.innerchildpress.com/the-year-of-the-poet

and there is much, much more !

visit . . .

www.innerchildpress.com/anthologies-sales-special.php

Also check out our Authors and all the wonderful Books Available at :

www.innerchildpress.com/authors-pages

World Healing World Peace
2020

Poets for Humanity

Now Available

www.worldhealingworldpeacepoetry.com

Now Available

www.worldhealingworldpeacepoetry.com

www.worldhealingworldpeacepoetry.com

World Healing
World Peace

2012, 2014, 2016, 2018, 2020

Now Available

www.worldhealingworldpeacepoetry.com

Inner Child Press International

'building bridges of cultural understanding'

Meet the Board of Directors

William S. Peters, Sr.
Chair Person
Founder
Inner Child Enterprises
Inner Child Press

Hülya N Yılmaz
Director
Editing Services
Co-Chair Person

Fahredin B. Shehu
Director
Cultural Affairs

Elizabeth E. Castillo
Director
Recording Secretary

De'Andre Hawthorne
Director
Performance Poetry

Gail Weston Shazor
Director
Anthologies

Kimberly Burnham
Director
Cultural Ambassador
Pacific Northwest
USA

Ashok K. Bhargava
Director
WIN Awards

Deborah Smart
Director
Publicity
Marketing

www.innerchildpress.com

This Anthological Publication
is underwritten solely by

Inner Child Press International

Inner Child Press is a Publishing Company Founded and Operated by Writers. Our personal publishing experiences provides us an intimate understanding of the sometimes daunting challenges Writers, New and Seasoned may face in the Business of Publishing and Marketing their Creative "Written Work".

For more Information

Inner Child Press International

www.innerchildpress.com

Inner Child Press International

'building bridges of cultural understanding'

202 Wiltree Court, State College, Pennsylvania 16801

www.innerchildpress.com

~ *fini* ~

www.ingramcontent.com/pod-product-compliance
Lightning Source LLC
LaVergne TN
LVHW010054110826
845155LV00028B/337